ON NATIONALISM AND COMMUNALISM IN INDIA

Randhir Singh

ON NATIONALISM AND COMMUNALISM IN INDIA
Randhir Singh

First Published, 2010

ISBN 978-93-5002-087-6 (Hb)

Published by
AAKAR BOOKS
28 E Pocket IV, Mayur Vihar Phase I, Delhi-110 091
Phone : 011-2279 5505 Telefax : 011-2279 5641
aakarbooks@gmail.com; www.aakarbooks.com

Printed at
Mudrak, Delhi-110 091

Publisher's Note

We have here put together three early writings of Professor Randhir Singh on the topical issues of Nationalism and Communalism in India. The author regrets the awkward repetition in the argument of these pieces and seeks the reader's indulgence, though, he says, a justification is not to be entirely ruled out. As Gunter Grass once put it: "In politics you have to repeat and repeat, like a parrot, ideas you know to be correct and proven as such, which is exhausting — you constantly hear the echo of your own voice and end up sounding like a parrot even to yourself. But this is evidently part of the job, if one has to find any listeners at all in a world so full of different voices."

K K Saxena

Contents

Chapter 1

Of Nationalism in India*

Yesterday, Today and Tomorrow

The thinker's function, to contribute our share to the description of reality, to improve (so far as we may) the modes of getting things chosen and done. This is everybody's guarantee of honour in other people's thoughts. It is the sole true objectivity, namely, a bias in favour of mankind. —Barrows Dunham

I deem it an honour to be asked to speak on this occasion, associated as it is with the name of Premchand who was an inspiration, in literature and otherwise, for my generation as we came of age in the late thirties and early forties when India's struggle for freedom stood poised to enter its final, most critical phase. Despite a certain well justified distrust of its leadership among us, there was a hopeful turbulence in the atmosphere around us. Premchand was, in his own way, a part of this turbulence and hopefulness of our nationalism.

I have been asked to speak on 'nation and nationalism'. With euphoria over Kargil still gripping the country, this is perhaps not the best of times to speak on this subject the way I propose to speak. But the issues involved, basic and

* Public lecture on Premchand's birth anniversary (July 31, 1999) at a meeting convened by the periodical *Hans*. Originally published in *Mainstream*, August 14, 1999.

urgent as ever, go beyond Kargil, and if one would function as an intellectual (as distinct from 'intellect worker') one cannot but be a critic of things in these our, in many ways, 'dark times'. As for Kargil, even as one admires the courage and dedication of the soldiers, one cannot resist thinking: what kind of politics between nations is this, rather between the ruling classes of our two nations, which sends hundreds of fellow human beings to their death on those barren hills and brings new miseries and sufferings to many more hundreds whom they leave behind on both sides of the border? Incidentally, even the best of conventional answers on both sides come befuddled with 'opium of patriotic feelings', as Marx once described it.

I am not going in for any scholary discourse on 'nation and nationalism' which necessarily needs to take note of the recent writings of Benedict Anderson, Gellner, Hobsbawm, Wallerstein-Balibar and others. I no longer have the kind of interest in the subject which, as a practising academic, I once had when concerns of peer-group scholarship had to be, necessarily, my concerns too. However, for most part of my 78 years, I have had another, a more alive concern with the subject, namely, with Indian nation and nationalism and it is one basic argument about it—based on what I have been speaking and writing in recent years—which I want to share with you this morning. If this is seen as a political rather than a 'scholarly'— whatever that means—exercise, I will only say that it is intended. Politics is where answers to the problems facing our people are to be found. It is indeed *the* arena of Indian people's struggle for their future. (It is a significant achievement of the ruling class politicians that, while their 'democratic politics' has failed to deliver so far as the people are concerned, they have managed to give politics itself a dirty name and thus helped better secure their system against revolutionary politics as well.)

Bhagat Singh's has always been a compelling presence

for me. His heroic figure loomed large over my childhood. A morning is still vividly etched on my mind, the morning after he and his comrades were hanged. I was detained, briefly, while passing in front of the Lahore Central Jail on my way to the primary school in the neighbourhood. The army and the police, a surging sea of humanity, tears in each eye and the proud faces, portraits, of the martyrs everywhere—and the defiant unending cry of '*Inquilab Zindabad*'... (Years later I was to spend a few months, among the happiest in my life, in the 'Terrorist Ward' of this very prison with some of the surviving comrades of Bhagat Singh who had in the meantime, like me, joined the Communist Party.) Nineteen thirty-nine onwards, alongwith these comrades of Bhagat Singh, I had the opportunity to work with the legendary survivors of the uprising of 1914-15 (and its other successors in the Ghadr movement) who had, almost naturally, moved on to Marxism and revolutionary socialism in their search for answers to the problems of their country. These were men who had competed with each other to defy death and mount the gallows with a smile, spent long, very long years, the best years of their life, in prisons of India and the Andamans, in solitary confinement and iron cages, chained to walls and ever in handcuffs, bars and fetters, and subjected to every conceivable torture, men who yet never gave in—bleeding but dignified, they suffered but fought on. And once out of their prisons, unbroken and unbowed, they rejoined the battle and carried on the same way, openly or underground, in prisons again or outside, till 1947—and I must add, to the very end, after 1947 too, after India became free and passed into the hands of new, now Indian rulers! What vision these revolutionaries had, what giants of human beings they were in their lifelong commitment to the cause of the Indian people! The contrast with the myopic pygmies who have today inherited this country is only too starkly obvious. And this does not preclude those on the Left who claim or are supposed to be their rightful heirs. This long-suffering land of ours, much too tired today, does not produce this breed of men any more ....It was indeed a privilege for me to be actively associated with these men—Bhagat Singh's comrades and the Ghadrite revolutionaries—who sought to move through a 'national' struggle for India's freedom to a social revolution in the country which makes possible for their countrymen a life worthy of human beings. Theirs was a dream and an inspiration which have stayed with me throughout my life.

In making a reference to this association of mine, apart from indicating the nature of my concern with the problematic of nationalism, I have a more specific purpose. During those heady, rebel days in the late sixties, students of Paris used to ask of everyone who would address them to first tell them: 'Where do you speak from?' A most legitimate question which I had learnt to answer rather early in my academic career when I discovered that I was perhaps the only teacher with a 'bias' at Delhi University—others were assumed to be objective, impartial, truly academic simply because they were not even aware of this question concerning one's philosophy, the prior philosophical-political position that everyone has and no one, literally no one, can do without—the position from which one inescapably speaks, and which therefore also needs to be honestly avowed. As for myself, within my broader philosophical-political preferences (which owe much to classical Marxism), it is from the standpoint of the above-referred revolutionary tradition of Indian nationalism which found an eloquent expression in Bhagat Singh who, charged with 'waging war against the King', had said that this war will go on 'so long as the Indian toiling masses are exploited by a handful of exploiters, be they purely British, or British and Indian in alliance, or even purely Indian'—that I am going to speak.

Notwithstanding the immense amount of scholarship expended on the subject, 'nation' remains, to borrow a description from Wallerstein-Balibar, 'an ambiguous identity'. But however 'ambiguous' an identity, or even an 'imagined community' of Benedict Anderson, nation, and with it nationalism, is nevertheless real enough to inspire or persuade individuals to die for their country. It is not, however; what nationalist ideologues tend to believe, even if their theory is not always explicit about it: some kind of supra-historical force, a Hegelian Absolute, as it were, at work in history, free of or in any case superior to all class or historical limitations, moving inevitably to a predestined end, the pride and glory of a self-realised nationhood in a nation-state. Hence the rhetoric over India as 'a nation' or the more fashionable 'a nation-in-the making', which is oblivious of the possibility that left to the ruling classes India may well be on its way to be 'a nation-in-the unmaking'; or the setting up of 'national unity and integrity' as an absolute value rather than defending it as a contingent *favourable condition* for the Indian people's struggle for a better future. Nationalism, instead of being treated as a phenomenon in need of historical explanation, tends to be treated as the prime explanatory principle of past or contemporary social and historical processes in India.

As against such or similar ahistorical conceptualisations, we do know that it is particular objective conditions or developments (economic, political, cultural, and still other) which combine to constitute and shape such or similar subjective identities as meaningful in society, making them terms for individual self-definition or identification and diffusing them across population sufficiently to turn them into objective social components of society which react back to themselves affect social conditions or developments—the subjective identities coming to play an objective role, for better or worse, in social and historical processes. For the purpose of my argument we need to recognise only this indisputable fact, namely, a most powerful social, political and ideological force of our times, nationalism is yet a historical phenomenon, with class and society-specific character, potentialities and limitations, and uses, and thus capable of manifesting itself in a variety of forms. Located as we are in the Third World and with the still-alive, though rapidly fading, memories of the long struggle against imperialism, we in this country are conventionally inclined to see nationalism as a liberationist force or ideology. But we will do well to remember that during the same period ruling classes of the countries of imperialism were finding nationalism useful not only to consolidate their rule at home but also to defend and justify their aggression and domination abroad. More recently, we have witnessed several cases of similar political-ideological use of nationalism by ruling class politicians—among these by Margaret Thatcher in England with the Falklands War which routed the Labour Party as never before, or by Ronald Reagan in the US in his twice successful bid for the American Presidency. Nearer home we saw Rajiv Gandhi romp home in the unprecedented electoral triumph of 1984 on a platform of nationalism, with strong Hindu chauvinist, even anti-Sikh, overtones—the emerging platform of Hinduised Indian nationalism, which has now been well and properly appropriated by another political formation of the Indian ruling classes, the Bharatiya Janata Party. And these days we hear of a desperate Yeltsin and quite a few of his equally desperate opponents turning to Russian national chauvinism as a diversionary device to retain or gain control over a deeply discontented and restive Russian people:... Besides, we must not forget that our times have witnessed the all too murderous nationalism of German, Japanese and Italian varieties. With the ruling classes, in the normal pursuit of their interests or when faced with situations of crisis in the polity, nationalism has often taken, all sorts of anti-people statist or racist or fascist or imperialist forms, providing ideological support or cover to the emergence of reactionary authoritarian regimes. And far too often in our times, people have been sacrificed to the 'nation'. All this apart, not only has fascism generally arrived in tandem with nationalism of one kind or the other, it is significant that Rightists, in power or out of it, have always claimed and monopolised nationalism as their own and manipulated it for their purposes. 'Nation', 'nationalism', 'national unity and integrity', 'patriotism', even 'the people', have been a loud part of the rhetoric of Right-wing politics everywhere, including the Third World.

Thus, understood in historical terms, nationalism is not in itself progressive or reactionary, secular or communal, democratic or authoritarian, anything better or worse. It all depends upon its specific character, its programme and leadership and, above all, concrete historical context and conjuncture. Such are the factors which determine its precise nature and historical role. Nationalism in India before 1947 was indeed progressive; under a different, more advanced class leadership and programme, it could have been radical, even revolutionary. It was progressive because it aimed at resolving .the basic structural contradictions of Indian society, congealed in imperialism, whose resolution, *against* imperialism, alone could clear the path for Indian people's continuing struggle for a better future. But nationalism need not be necessarily or entirely so in the post-1947 period. For the settlement of 1947 had its own harsh logic. It is customary in conventional scholarship or historiography to take a liberal, linear view of the historical process in India around and after 1947. In this view the Indian nation, or 'nation-in-the-making' if you prefer, is seen as winning *political* freedom for India in 1947, and then, expectedly and almost unproblematically, moving on to win *economic* freedom for the country—a movement which more than fifty years hence is still on. The real historical process, however, has been quite different, essentially dialectical. The very manner in which the contradictions with imperialism were resolved, its 'transfer of power' involving no basic economic or social structural change, but putting new, now *Indian* ruling classes in control of the state power—this made the India people's struggle for economic freedom not only that much more complex and difficult but also primarily a matter of struggle against these classes. For it is here, *within* the nation, that the basic structural contradictions of Indian society now come to be located as the new rulers use their newly won state power to facilitate a historically specific form of capitalist development in the country, even as they continue to maintain, with due modifications, the old exploitative and oppressive socio-economic structures of Indian society. While continuing to be an inspiration for the people to rebuild their just-liberated country, nationalism or a nationalist perspective can now also serve to obscure the class character of the settlement of 1947 and its outcome.

A structural cognition or mapping of Indian society will reveal this outcome as an India-specific capitalism—'a type of capitalist development in the interests of a narrow section of Indian society' as V K R V Rao saw it—whose structural logic of unequal and uneven development has led to the emergence of the now universally admitted 'two nations' (the rich and the poor)—the Indian 'twin-nation' (K N Raj), 'socio-economic *dualism*' which is so very 'corrosive' (Sukhamoy Chakravarty), 'this dualism in Indian society' which is threatening to become 'explosive' (V K R V Rao), the 'two Indias' of Rajni Kothari, V P Singh, R K Hegde *et al.*, etc.—and a certain 'internal colonialism' in relation to the more backward parts of the country. Its historical specificity has given it a strong comparador or *secondary* character, presided over as it is by a bourgeoisie born old without every having known youth, with none of the possible virtues of youth and all the vices of old age. Here all the exploitative and oppressive evils of belated capitalist development, semi-feudalism, bureaucratically corrupt public sector and bloated bourgeois politics daily enter into and reinforce each other. Karl Marx had once written: 'As is well known, secondary diseases are more difficult to cure and at the same time, ravage the body more than original ones.' Which is as good an explanation as any of the myriad economic, social and moral ills ravaging our society today. Every aspect of social life in India bears the signature of this historically specific Indian form of capitalist development—its mark is there on our morality, our culture, our politics, on everything, everywhere. Therefore, if there is indeed a 'national mainstream'—which somebody or the other is all the time being invited to join or rejoin, as if some morality play is on—it is, bearing the impress of India's corrupt and corrupting, somewhat lumpen capitalist development, an increasingly dirty affair—corrupt, communal and criminalised, a repressively homogenising, mainstream. As for 'national integration', the fact to be deplored is not that we are not integrated but that we are integrated the *capitalist* way which, by its very nature, carries strong dsintegrative tendencies within it and has today made all the divides and fissures of Indian society—around class, caste or religion, language, ethnicity or nationality; etc.—sharper and potentially explosive. Outside of economy it has been a case of the 'state as private property', and any kind of power in the state as a means of 'rapid private accumulation'; democracy, fought for and won by the people, still valuable to them, and throughout defended by them against subversion from above, yet only vindicates Bagehot's classic observation about its being 'the way to give the people the greatest illusion of power while allowing them the smallest amount in reality'; and 'democratic politics' has steadily degenerated into an utterly unscrupulous, no-holds-barred infighting among the beneficiaries of the system for power and pelf in the state, where as they violate the rules of their own game, it is now truly the end justifying the means, literally any means (including rank communalism)....

Such being the situation, it is not only that in a society torn with extremes of socio-economic inequality and conflicting class interests, to postulate 'common national interests', a 'national good' shared by all citizens, is a most tenuously abstract and deceptive notion or that this abstraction is capable of serving as an ideological device to deny or disguise, to disaggregate and delegitimise, at least depoliticise, other daily experienced identities and solidarities in society, most importantly its basic class identities and solidarities; or that aspirations growing out of the rich mosaic of India's diversity and plurality, especially those of its oppressed collectivities, minority groups or nationalities can be viewed as so many challenges to India's 'unity and integrity' and, alongwith people's other challenges from below, denounced as 'anti-national' and sought to be suppressed; or that, when their policies end up generating major crises for the system, nationalism well serves the rulers in their ideological manipulation of the people: the bogey of 'secessionism', 'destablisation', 'threat to unity and integrity of India', etc. is invoked to divert people away from their own concerns and mobilise them behind ruling class politics, to silence dissent as 'unpatriotic', to delegitimise popular struggles as inopportune in the prevailing supposedly temporary situations and secure public sanction to further expand and strengthen the repressive state apparatuses for use against the people and a better defence of the general interests of the ruling classes—and so on. Basic to it all is the overarching fact that nationalism or a nationalist perspective—with its wide array of supportive concepts like 'national economy' or 'national development'; 'nation-building' or 'state-building', 'national mainstream', 'national integration' or 'unity and integrity of the nation', etc.—conceals the essential character of Indian social reality as it has come to be as a result of an India specific capitalist development. Nationalism not only serves to cover up, or provide alibis for, the historical default of the post-colonial ruling classes in India, it increasingly turns into a legitimising ideology for these classes in need of defending and safeguarding their economic and political domination. One political formation of the ruling classes has even come up with a Hindu-chauvinist nationalism, 'cultural nationalism' as they call it, to gain popular support and in the name of '*swadeshi*' better defend and promote the interests of India's 'national' capitalism.

By obscuring the most basic division in our society, between *us* (the people) and *them* (who exploit and oppress), nationalism permits the latter even to get away with plain lies to justify and gather support for their policies and politics. Witness, for example, the lie that was the well-orchestrated national chorus to launch the recent class-interests' dictated 'new economic policy' or surrender to global capitalism: 'the country has been living beyond its means'. For a good majority of our people have simply no means at all to live, and most others nothing much to indulge any 'living beyond'. The nationalist lie provides a cover for those who have indeed been living beyond this country's poor means for long, via a government supported capitalism, and are now set on continuing to do so via the 'free market' capitalism, those whom the Latin Americans have learnt to call 'anti-nation within the nation.'

I regard the success or failure of the Left in our country a matter of decisive importance for the future of our people, and the Communist Parties constitute the most vital part of the Left forces in India today. It is important to note therefore that a simplistic and unthinking, essentially ahistorical nationalism, the internalising of a nationalist as against a Marxist perspective for its theory and practice in the post-independence period, has virtually disarmed the mainstream Communist Left ideologically, depriving it of the 'independent political position' that Marx always emphasised and Lenin repeatedly endorsed as absolutely necessary for revolutionary politics. Joining in the competitive nationalism of the dominant bourgeois politics, speaking the same language and loud-mouthing the same slogans of 'national development', 'national integration', 'national mainstream', 'unity and integrity of India', and sharing the same fears of 'destablisation' etc. etc., has led this Left again and again to an 'appealing' or 'deploring', more or less active, tailist alignment with one or the other ruling class political formation, often helplessly advising those in power with 'wise' and 'sensible' solutions to problems of their own creation, which 'solutions' are invariably ignored or rebuffed by the latter as they go on to create new problems and further mess up the old ones. A 'nationalist' blurring of the distinction between bourgeois and socialist politics has taken place, with the consequence that the ruling class politics has always succeeded in effectively defining and pre-empting the terrain of Indian politics, setting the parameters of intellectual discourse and political action, imposing its own issues and choices, concepts, language codes and forms of politics on others, in the process appropriating, marginalising, and suppressing whenever necessary, those of any kind of alternative radical or revolutionary politics, which has thus survived only at the fringes of Indian polity. 'Nationalism' has helped the ruling classes and their political representatives to ensure that the larger context and the deeper determinant inter-connections of social reality are obscured and the issues or problems dissociated from all considerations of class structure, class domination, or ruling class politics, enabling them to push the people's genuine interests out of the picture, alongwith all radical or revolutionary choices—these are simply not allowed to arise as real, historical possibilities. Given their internalisation of a nationalist perspective, the mainstream Communist Parties have been by and large content with operating on the terrain of bourgeois politics only, reacting or responding to the issues it presents, accepting the choices it offers, and succumbing to the corruption of consciousness all this involves, in the process not only getting marginalised again and again but also losing their character, the revolutionary commitment and elan that define a party as Communist. (A most serious theoretical disorientation on the Communist Left has been to see socialism itself, on the rare occasions they still speak of it, as an adjunct of national aspirations, which leaves socialism very much an utopian affair. But this is not a theme I need to pursue here.)

Lenin had drawn attention to the bourgeoisie's 'striving to fortify nationalism' in its interest. This striving has been very much a part of India's ruling class politics especially in the crisis-ridden recent decades. And more the crisis deepens, discontents mount, disruption or disorder spreads and the ruling class legitimacy gets undermined, louder become the exhortations in the name of nationalism or patriotism. And as these exhortations are increasingly recognised as so many cliches, as nationalism continues to wane and patriotism grows tired and flabby, they are sought to be flogged into some semblance of life or movement, through the media controlled by the corporates or the state, through editorials and advertisements in the press, through wayside hoardings (*mera Bharat mahan*, etc.) and interminable singing; and running for the country on the television and elsewhere, through the rhetoric of politicians and, the laboured theorising of in-house scholars and through extravaganzas, *utsavs* and centenaries of all sorts... As Marx had suggested 'opium of patriotic feeling' is indeed useful to the rulers for securing their class interests. (I may add that love for the Indian people, for India's glorious heritage through the ages, including those magnificent expressions of our people's creativity in the then inevitable religious idiom, or a *socialist* commitment to the unity and interests of the Indian people and an abiding faith in their future—all this certainly does not require this opiate.)

I will conclude this part of my argument with a brief reference to an interesting and instructive linguistic practice in the contemporary nationalist discourse in our country—its almost obsessive use of the term 'unfortunate'. Those who argue in the nationalist mode in their scholarship or historiography or politics, whenever they are confronted with certain unpleasant facts or practices, inadequacies or limitations, defaults or failures of Indian nationalism, nationalist politics or leadership—in relation to communalism or land reforms, for example—they invariably tend to rationalise them as something 'unfortunate'. Now there may be some justification for this linguistic practice while speaking of events in the immediate present when, within the necessities of a given objective situation, politics is still a realm of possibilities, of choices to be made, and therefore the choices being made legitimately open to judgement not only on empirical or scientific grounds but on meaningful ethical or moral grounds as well. But once a particular possibility has been realised and the choices are closed, once the deed is done and it is discovered to be 'unfortunate', the real task, in my view, is a historical materialist explanation of what actually came to pass. The nationalist perspective has a persistent tendency to evade this task and rest content with the moral judgment, unfortunate, as if this was also an adequate empirical explanation of what happened. This linguistic practice not only condones the historic defaults or failures of Indian nationalism, nationalist politics or leadership, but also obscures their ultimate basis in the class and history determined character of this nationalism, nationalist politics or leadership.

I have spoken of things past and present in relation to nationalism in India. Let me now use this past and present to offer an argument about the future. India's struggle for freedom was a major 'meta-narrative' of our times. Before 1947, we were part of a global system, well-integrated into a world market economy. We were globalised, so to speak, but we did not like it. Our globalisation then also had a name, imperialism, and we struggled against it, precisely because its structural logic meant the accumulation of wealth in England and poverty in India. Like other Third World countries we wanted to get out of this globalisation to be able to opt for an independent, self-reliant development in the interests of our common people. Herein lay the essential meaning of our long struggle for freedom.

We won our freedom in 1947. To understand what really happened in this historic event, it helps to think of what did not happen at the time. There was no revolutionary overthrow of the British imperialist rule in India, no accompanying economic or social or even political revolution. The Gandhi-bourgeois led freedom struggle (a defensible and better description than any other) ended in a compromise and settlement with imperialism which transferred political power from the foreign rulers to the Indian rulers, leaving the old socio-economic and state-bureaucratic structures largely intact which, in turn, with all their structural compulsions, became the basis for the post-colonial 'national development'. This development has carried the full impress of the way freedom was finally 'won' in 1947.

The post-colonial rulers in India, having gained power

in the state, went on to set up a 'national project' of self-reliant economic development to supplement the recently won political freedom with the more important economic freedom for the Indian people. The Soviet Union, its lack of democracy apart, was seen as an example of successful state intervention in economy (which the Indian bourgeoisie itself deemed necessary), the Cold War allowed the new rulers a certain manoeuvrability of action, and Nehru's 'socialistic pattern of society', to be achieved through parliamentary means, soon provided the necessary ideological underpinning for the post-colonial process of national reconstruction, with its focus on the state sector to build up the economy, affirmative action for the most disadvantaged sections of society and economic growth in general which was to benefit the people at large. The project was not lacking in vision and it soon had significant achievements to its credit. But despite Nehru's awareness of the 'terrible costs of not changing the existing order', this project was no radical break with 'the existing order', vindicating Marx who had, in his analysis of the failed German revolution of 1848, already said that henceforth the bourgeoisie could not be relied upon to make success of even a bourgeois democratic revolution.

The Nehru era was the golden age of India's 'national project', though it was never without its critics. The slogan was 'growth with equity and distributive justice' for the people. Acting as 'the executor of the economic necessities of the national situation', as Engels once put it, the Indian state indeed ensured growth in the economy but the hope for justice to people was largely belied. The years that followed revealed the inherent limitations of the Nehruvian national project. It was fast ending up as a class project—an India-specific capitalism that we have noticed earlier—but was not recognised as such. It had its beneficiaries, and there was a consensus of the arrived and the complacent about it. Nationalism too had its uses, the emerging reality could be obscured in its name. Such was the domination of the ruling class ideas that even those who saw capitalism, saw it more as our very own 'national economy'; and, together with faith and force of habit, it ensured the prevalence of the view that the 'national project' was still on. But there was nothing much in it for the vast masses of the common Indian people. To borrow from Tom Paine's metaphoric rejoinder to Burke's attack on the French Revolution, the 'plumage' of India's 'national development' was yet that of a 'dying bird'. The world looked very different from below, when the poor and oppressed of 'our nation' looked at it. However, the definitive collapse of the national project was still in the future.

Mid-sixties onwards the post-colonial national project in India floundered and fast degenerated, its economic crises underpinning and moving in step with the crises of the political system, 'democratic politics' and all that. If India's 'national economy' generated any number of potentially explosive issues, its 'national politics' regularly turned these issues into problems, problems into running sores and these sores into tragedies for the Indian people, in Punjab, Kashmir, almost everywhere. By the end of the eighties the national project was virtually over. Soon enough a dead-end economic crisis or financial bankruptcy of sorts, produced by the previously pursued policies, coincided with the defeat of the Soviet Union in the Cold War and its eventual disintegration, depriving the Indian ruing classes of whatever little manoeuvrability they still had and leaving them more vulnerable than ever before to the offensive of a recharged global capitalism. Given the strong comprador or lumpen strain inherent in their character, led by their major political formation, the Congress-I, with their other political formations in tow, they succumbed, and hiccups and protests notwithstanding, opted for what is turning out to be a junior partnership within the global capitalist system. As beneficiaries of 'growth' during the Nehru era and afterwards, and now with a substantial economic strength of their own, globalisation also provides them, with new avenues of profit making at home and abroad. Therefore, this 'succumbing' can also be seen as a natural progress for Indian capitalism. India was again globalised, this time through a largely voluntary submission of the Indian rulers. The national project finally and definitively collapsed in 1991.

The evidence of this collapse is there in the disintegration of values and degradation of life all around us, in the continuing poverty of our people and growing consumerism of the elites and a society at once cynical and fearful about the future. It is there in official statistics and pages of the private media, in our 'two nations', 'internal colonialism' and the corrupt, communal and criminalised 'national mainstream'. The evidence is there in the visionless and so obviously laboured efforts of the powers-that-be to yet again flog a tired and flabby patriotism into some semblance of life that characterised the celebrations of the fiftieth anniversary of India's independence and included a Colgate-sponsored selling of *Vande Matrams* on the television by 'distinguished Indian citizens' as they are called. And this evidence is pathetically present in the impotence (or is it hypocrisy?) of the supposedly 'stirring' calls made on the occasion—in Parliament for a 'second freedom struggle' and by the Prime Minister to 'begin the struggle for economic freedom'! One wonders about the freedom we are supposed to have won fifty years ago and what these past fifty years have been about. A Finance Minister asking us to forget, not fear, the East India Company, opened up India to the multinationals, that is, took India back into globalisation on the dishonest plea that 'the nation has been living beyond its means'—'nation' indeed, when a good majority of our people have simply no means to live and most others none to indulge any 'living beyond'! His successor, more honest and ideologically committed, publicly pleaded with the former globalisers in London, successors of the East India Company, to come back to India for another equally long stay (and then went to town with this pleading in Washington and elsewhere): 'You came to India and stayed for 200 years. Now come prepared to invest and stay for another 200 years, and there will be huge rewards,' The post-colonial 'national project' was indeed over and done with.

Capitalism is today so powerful and pervasive as to have become invisible, and it is all the more powerful for being invisible. You no longer mention or recognise it. It is there, but without a name as it were, a harmless, nay benevolent, phenomenon called 'globalisation', recently arrived on the world scene to help the poor and backward countries out of their problems. Globalisation, nevertheless, has a proper name, capitalism, its world economy or market is a capitalist world economy or market. Harvard economist Robert Reich's phrase 'secession of the successful' is vividly expressive of a crucial feature of any capitalist market society. Globalisation of India means that the 'successful' of Indian society, the ruling elites of India, have decided to 'secede' from the common Indian people—even a cursory look at the former's values, life-style and culture today makes this abundantly clear. A capitalist market society is also a case of 'the economy is doing fine, the people are not', as a former President of Brazil once reported it to the masters in Washington. Therefore, the Indian economy may do 'fine' (with its growth rates, etc.) but, given its *structural logic*, the Indian people will not; for them the consequences of the current globalisation are not likely to be much different from those of the globalisation they had struggled hard and long to finally escape in 1947. Their peripheralisation this time could well be much worse.

The 'national project' having collapsed, the ruling classes

of India have, through their different political formations, decided to 'secede' from the people and opted for 'globalisation' as their strategic option for the future. The Indian people once again face the question, whose full implications were somewhat obscured in 1947, due largely to the interim successes of the Soviet Union (since sucked back into global capitalism): what do they do in the current situation of global domination of capitalism? The historical experience in India and elsewhere in the Third World makes it abundantly clear that they will find no answers in capitalism, national or globalised. The choice for them remains socialism or peripheralisation in the global capitalist system. This is not to posit socialism as achievable today or tomorrow, or even the day-after for that matter, but to posit a socialism-oriented autonomous development as people's strategic option (against the ruling classes' strategic option of globalisation) wherein socialism as the principle governing an alternative people's politics links together their immediate, ongoing and emerging struggles in an *ultimate* project of revolutionary transformation of our society and is the goal of a long transitional process, whose specifics and speed will depend upon the objective material conditions and the nature and balance of the class forces involved at each stage of the struggle. Immediately, it means saying 'no' to globalisation: This is not to argue for any kind of 'autarky' in economic development but to pose the issue of whether this development will be governed by *external* imperatives, those issuing from the requirements of the world capitalist market (export-led growth, etc.) and the associated consumerism of the rich, or primarily by *internal* imperatives, those flowing from an assessment of our own resources and the needs of our people.

The issue, in other words, is that of priorities: development for what and whom? Is it to satisfy the basic needs of the people or the consumerism of the elite in our society? The argument is for a pro-people socialism-oriented endogenous development which draws on our own strengths, our domestic resources and capacities, including those of the hard working poor who still remain the most creative and productive in our society, a development which gives the common people, in both urban and rural areas, a positive stake in the economy and mobilises them for building a better society and, let me add, for the inevitable struggle against global imperialism and its local allies or partners. This has to be the alternative strategic option of the Indian people.

Technological backwardness is often pressed as an argument to counter the plea for such autonomous economic development in a Third World country. Here, apart from the fact that in India at least we are not that lacking in either technology or the talent for it, we need to overcome the widely prevalent fetishism of science and technology, which at times (as, for example, with Nehru and his 'temples of modern India', etc.) has even gone to the extent of expecting them to do the job of a social revolution, which they simply cannot. As with economics so with technology, the question again is one of priorities: technology for what purpose? Once this question is asked, the argument for getting access to the most modem Western technology, via globalisation—even if that was certain which it certainly is not—loses much of its force. If the purpose is to satisfy the consumerist hunger of the privileged part of our population with the most modern gadgets and designs, and the goodies of the West, then rushing into globalisation indeed makes some sense. But if the purpose or priority is to meet the needs of all the people for decent food, clothing and shelter, clean water, proper sanitation and health protection, education and cultural opportunities; and the like, then devoting scarce resources to the most modem technology is simply wasteful, because there is little in the latest technology of the West that could make a significant contribution. In fact what is most useful and relevant in technology, Western or otherwise, for improving the way of life of the masses is widely known; moreover most of it is already available at home and what else is needed, is obtainable in the normal course of managed trade.

A socialism-oriented autonomous economic development as a strategic option for our people is premised on *politics*, that is *people's politics* and not *'the market'* commanding the economy (which, however, does not rule out an useful role for the market). The crux of the matter therefore is people's power in the state, their 'political supremacy' in society, as Marx put it. Not a phoney 'empowerment' from above, but people fighting and winning power for themselves through their own struggles and then using it, through whatever democratic means are available and otherwise, to promote their own interests which are, in the final analysis, tied up with basic, economic-structural changes in society. This draws our attention to an important missing dimension of politics in the country today, where an essentially exhausted electoral democracy apart, a seemingly apolitical 'social activism', as it is called, has absorbed the energies of an unusually large number of well-meaning change-seeking individuals and organisations. A most welcome development and a witness to the multifaceted crisis in our society, contemporary 'social activism' is also indicative of the general absence of the more needed *radical politics* which seeks fundamental, structural changes in our society—for which reason, despite widespread social activism, the crisis in our society continues to deepen (and not unsurprisingly quite a few social activists, rewarded or otherwise, end up as decorations to the system and their activism as its legitimisation). What is needed in place of the present largely moralising understanding and activism but including it, is structural analysis and radical politics. Moral passion is central to any genuine pro-people activism, but by itself it generates only a most ephemeral and ineffectual kind of politics which is easily reabsorbed and recontained by the system and generally serves to legitimise it. It is historical experience that a moralising politics and its piecemeal activism (generally acceptable to the ruling classes) tends to develop when a structural cognition or mapping of society is blocked. Such cognition or mapping of Indian society is what our argument has been based upon. Only on this basis is it possible to argue for and practice radical politics aimed at securing people's power in the state for a socialism-oriented autonomous development in the country.

If such development is necessary in the interests of our people and they have no choice but to attempt it if they would avoid peripheralisation, with the people *really in power* it is also possible. The failure of the world's first experiment in socialism notwithstanding, there is much in its experience to help guide this attempt and be hopeful about it: for example, in the still unparalleled achievements of the early years of the post-revolutionary societies in Russia and elsewhere despite their economic backwardness, in Cuba's heroic struggle to save the gains of its socialist revolution, in Lenin's socialist project during the years that he survived the October Revolution, in the experience of the 'Mao years' in China ('leave agriculture but don't leave village' policies, etc.) and so on. An uncharted territory, we can still enter it with confidence.

With this let me return to the question of nationalism in India in relation to the future of our country. The post-colonial national project may have collapsed and, in terms of their objective interests, the paths of the ruling elite and the people may have diverged as never before, but nationalism yet remains a very strong sentiment among our people. Many of those who would agree with me may still regard the struggle for a socialism-oriented autonomous, economic development as a national struggle, a continuation; as it were, of the Indian people's earlier national struggle for freedom which has no doubt failed to deliver but pursued better may do so in future. Contributing to the confusion here is the notion of this struggle as 'national popular'—an increasingly fashionable concept which originated with Gramsci as part of his perspective for a socialist revolution in Italy involving an alliance between the working class and the peasantry, but now more associated with Samir Amin's perspective on people's (and not class-specific or socialist) revolutions of the periphery, revolutions viewed as the Third World peoples' 'national protection and self-assertion' against capitalist development which they find intolerable. Ignoring or obscuring the fact that nations in the Third World are today internally more or less sharply class-divided societies, that imperialism now finds willing collaborators in the post-colonial ruling classes or elites, that 'nationalism', whatever its other aspects or potentialities, is today a potent ideological weapon in the hands of these ruling classes and elites, such conceptualisation is seriously flawed as a perspective for the revolutionary processes in the Third World, including a country like India. As I have argued above, as against the pre-1947 situation, with the post-colonial rulers having facilitated a historically specific form of capitalist development in the country, the basic contradictions that now need to be resolved to clear the path for the Indian people's continuing struggle for a better life lie *within* the nation, and their resolution is primarily a matter of struggle within, against the Indian ruling classes; therefore, strictly speaking this struggle cannot be viewed simply as a national struggle. In fact the Indian people's continuing struggle against imperialism, globalisation's neo-colonialism too is now a part of this new struggle within, and not a continuation of the pre-1947 anti-imperialist struggle; because the neo-colonialist 'integration', rather reintegration, into the global capitalist economy is now occurring by the grace of, through the opportunities provided by, indeed at the invitation of, the new rulers at Delhi. Nationalism or a national perspective only obscures this most basic of all issues facing the Indian people.

Thus, the struggle for a people's strategic option as against 'globalisation' that the Indian ruling classes have opted for, the struggle for socialism-oriented autonomous development—which alone can also be an ecologically sustainable development as against a globalised Indian capitalism subject to the capital-accumulative or profit-making imperatives of the market—is not a national struggle as such, nor a continuation of the earlier national struggle in India, though it can be and needs to be seen as its transcendence in a strictly dialectical sense, that is, a struggle that carries forward the best traditions and hopes of the earlier liberationist struggles of the Indian people It is in its basic character a class struggle in the proper Marxian sense which eschews its narrow economistic or class-reductionist interpretations. No doubt a great deal of tactical resilience is necessary in relating it, theoretically as well as practically to the obviously important question of nationalism. But even if this struggle is viewed as a national or 'national-popular' struggle of the Indian people, it cannot but be fighting the 'anti-nation within the nation', as the Latin Americans now call 'it, or 'rescuing the nation' from its ruling classes, or, as Marx would have put it, the people 'establishing itself as the nation', and thus remains, in its essential content, a class struggle. It cannot be seen as a collective struggle of all the people in the post-colonial state for a common good and against a foreign power as, essentially the struggle for national liberation was; it will be, more than anything else, a struggle for political power, to win it from own ruling classes and for purposes entirely opposite to theirs. That is how the national task, recovering the country for its people, is now, as it were, also a class task of the Indian people, people acting as a 'nation class'; to borrow a description from the Guinean Marxist revolutionary, Cabral. Such has to be the perspective of the Indian people's struggle against globalisation and for a better life today. At the very least genuine nationalists must understand that our country's future is tied to the future of socialism in our country.

Chapter 2

Theorising Communalism in India*

A Fragmentary Note in the Marxist Mode

Communalism, in its diverse forms and expressions, including recurring riots, has emerged as an increasingly significant phenomenon, of a decisively negative kind, in Indian society and politics in recent years. Understandably, it has drawn the attention not only of the practitioners of politics of all hues but also of scholars in the universities, research institutes and elsewhere. A great deal of useful work has been done, providing us with a lot more information and insights concerning communalism and related issues than we had ever before. And this is most welcome for understanding communalism in contemporary India and for waging an effective struggle against it.

I

Most of this work, however, has remained, by and large, within the parameters of the dominant political thought of

* Originally published in *Economic & Political Weekly*, July 23, 1988. A comment concerning 'communalism' in 'Marxists and the Sikh Extremist Movement' (published by *EPW* earlier) provoked a demand for explanation from my young radical friends in Punjab. This note was written in response to that demand and dedicated to the memory of Moin Shakir.

the pre independence period in this country. Communalism was then perceived primarily as an imperialism instigated divisive and false doctrine and it was sought to be opposed variously in terms of idealist humanism, liberal rationalism, even 'true religion', and above all in terms of the emerging unifying ideology of nationalism. This was closely allied, especially on the Left, to an economic interpretation of communalism which hoped, *a la* Nehru and others, that 'economic development' will take care of the remaining problems that communalism posed. An important underlying principle of the liberal-left secularism of the period was the view that religion which fed or was manipulated to feed communalism was itself only an erroneous view of the cosmos which would in due course, as scientific thinking grows and economic development takes place, yield to a rational understanding of things. This was expected to undermine religion as one important source of communalism and help along the process of building a secular polity in India. (I am not here concerned with the dominant political practice of the national movement in this period which, Gandhi and bourgeois led as it was, sought communal unity or harmony, in the main, through deals or compromises at the top, between the elite leaders of different communities, but shied away from seeking it from below, through the militant unity of the Indian masses, of all communities, fighting together for their common national and class interests.)

Recent work on communalism, however, representing as it does an increasingly self conscious engagement with the problem, is noticeable for at least two features, having positive as well as negative aspects.

In the first place, study of communalism has become, as never before, an object of academic research, an organised enterprise in the universities and research institutes. This has meant more systematic work and also efforts at more rigorous thinking, and has significantly contributed to our knowledge and wisdom in this area. (As an example, we have the painstaking empirical studies of communal riots and disturbances.) At the same time, as a consequence of the 'functional rationality' that comes to govern every such enterprise, there is not only an increase in sheer quantitative output but also the growth of new, orthodoxies, of 'invisible colleges' and 'repute systems', of laboured theorising full of scholastic refinements, of definitions and distinctions, 'forms' and 'stages' galore. Thus, for example, along with the received notions ('majority communalism', 'minority communalism', etc.) we now have 'communal nationalism' (though we are also immediately informed: 'this form was, properly speaking, not communalism at all'), 'liberal communalism', 'extreme communalism' or 'fascist communalism', 'communalism conformist', 'communalism conformist and incremental', 'communalism-secessionist', and so on. We may expect more of this scholastic sophistication as academic research catches on, lending respectability of sorts to what is often only a 'common sense view of communalism in our country.

The second noticeable feature of recent scholarship on communalism is that it is much influenced by Marxism and a significant part of it even explicitly claims to be Marxist. Thus we have a profusion of references to 'economy', 'economic factors', 'social basis', 'socio-economic changes', even 'capitalism' or 'capitalist path of development', etc., and to the need in this connection for 'faster economic growth', 'radical economic changes', 'changing social reality', even 'socialist transformation', and so on. This again is a significant advance, drawing our attention to some of the more material or objective factors in the situation, and to the need for struggle against communalism in diverse fields and at more basic levels. However, references to it notwithstanding, most often Marxism has only a general or eclectic presence in this work, as something which is somehow or somewhere or the other *also* there.* It is never integral to the analysis of communalism as a significant part or aspect or instance of the Indian social whole. What we have is, at best, yet again, exercises in economic interpretation which, it is well to remember, is as old as Plato; at times it is plain economic reductionism, as when a scholar writes: 'communalism today is the product of capitalism which is not able to develop the society fast enough to meet the needs of that society.' (The implied assumption about capitalism's ability 'to develop society', fast enough or otherwise, or its concern for 'the needs of society' is hardly deserving of serious comment.) In this genre of work we often find, as in the pre-independence period, an eclectic combination of economic and ideological causation wherein soon, especially at the level of practice, it is ideology that comes to acquire primacy as the cause and cure of communalism—communalism, the divisive and false ideology to be overcome by the ideology of nationalism.

II

These are but some peripheral considerations regarding contemporary scholarship on communalism. This scholarship also suffers from several substantive weaknesses of approach to the study of communalism. In this note I am primarily concerned with only two of these which are relatively more significant from the point of view of theory as well as political practice. It seems to me that most contemporary thinking, writing or theorisation on

---

* Like 'h' in 'wheat'. The story relates to a student in my college days who went on to become a teacher of agriculture. His English was none too good. Asked to spell 'wheat' he answered 'w-e-a-t' and then, suddenly remembering, exclaimed: 'There is an 'h' also... an 'h' is also there!'

communalism, its achievements notwithstanding, is seriously flawed by an ideological error on the one hand and a methodological limitation on the other. The ideological error, which has virtually pre-emptied the entire field of thought or study on communalism in this country, lies in understanding communalism from the standpoint of nationalism. And the methodological limitation lies in studying contemporary communalism in an essentially empiricist and often ahistorical manner, a manner which, even as it has contributed much to social science research in recent times, has also in a way seriously crippled it. The two, the error and the limitation, have been generally mutually accommodative, sometimes eclectically, present in the work of the same scholar. While highlighting certain important dimensions of communalism in Indian social life and politics, particularly in relation to our freedom struggle, the nationalist mode or perspective, which sees it primarily, if not solely, as an anti-national phenomenon, can be most misleading in our efforts to understand contemporary communalism. And, while grasping its diverse and significant objective aspects, the empiricist method yet fails to provide a comprehensive understanding of communalism with all its interconnections as a determined and determining part of Indian social and political life today.

The dominance of the nationalist mode of thought in the study of communalism, as in many other areas of social analysis, is easily understandable in the historical context of India's long struggle for freedom from foreign rule, culminating in 'the final victory'—the compromise and the settlement of 1947. The attraction and usefulness of this mode for the now dominant Indian ruling classes which, in Gunnar Myrdal's words, did `little more than displace a foreign with a native privileged group', is only too obvious. For, in continuation of the past practice, quite legitimate then, this mode even now, explicitly or somewhat ambiguously, locates imperialism as the primary source of all our problems, including those relating to communalism. The nationalist perspective thus obscures the all important distinction between the essentially indigenous creation of most of these problems and imperialism's contribution to and taking advantage of these for its own ends.

The nationalist mode or perspective sees 1947 as the triumph of Indian nationalism and perceives communalism as something subversive or disruptive of this nationalism, now seeking to consolidate, to more fully realise itself. And if communalism is defined to be 'above all' an ideology, as many scholars have indeed done, the struggle against it is sought to be waged in terms of the counter ideology of nationalism. Implicit in this mode or perspective is the view that regards nationalism not as a historical phenomenon but as some supra historical force, an Hegelian Absolute as it were, now at work in Indian History, free of or in any case superior to all class or historical limitations, and moving almost inevitably to a predetermined end—a self realised, fully integrated Indian nationhood. The concerned scholars, especially historians among them, may have once upon a time viewed Indian nationalism as a phenomenon in need of a historical explanation. But caught up in their own essentially ahistorical conceptualisations—'nation-in-the-making', etc.—they now seem to argue as if nationalism itself is the prime explanatory principle of contemporary social and historical process in India.

No doubt, Marxism, classical as well as contemporary, has its problems with nationalism, among the most important phenomena of modern times—problems at the level of both theory and practice. It was and remains a complex relationship, indeed a 'difficult dialogue' between them. Marxism certainly still lacks a coherent theory of nationalism, of nations, nationalities and national minorities. More specifically, Marxism in India has yet to come to terms with the reality of Indian nationalism, as it has to with so many other specificities of the Indian social formation—what with its size and the complex contradictions-laden dimensions of history and social life, economy and ecology, class, caste and gender, thought and culture, religion and language, ethnicity and nationality, and so on. The need for such a theory is especially urgent today in view of the significant re-emergence of the problem of nationalities and ethnic groups in our country, particularly the minor and more dis-advantaged ones, which, subject to exploitation and oppression, old and new and at several levels, are today struggling to win justice and find a place of dignity and honour among the Indian people. These struggles or movements, asserting the right to autonomy, or even statehood, are expressive of the genuine aspirations of the oppressed people; and they are emerging in the ultimate analysis on the material basis of a capitalist development which has meant not only exploitation and oppression of the people but also unequal and uneven development in the country as a whole. In the absence of an adequate theory-based practice, there will be a strong tendency to be opportunist, or at best, only instrumentalist, in one's approach to these struggles or movements. We need a theory and practice that will help us articulate these struggles with the class struggles of the exploited and the oppressed, to infuse them with socialist concerns. For unless this is done, they may only breed local chauvinism and authoritarian practices replicating what is happening at the national level, divide the people and disrupt their actual or potential common struggles and end up serving the interests of the locally dominant exploiting classes and other vested interests seeking a place for themselves within India's underdeveloped capitalism and overdeveloped bourgeois politics.

However, I am not here interested in a discussion of these general questions of nationalism and Marxist theory. My immediate concern is with the limited issue of the nationalist perspective on communalism. And my basic argument is that while one must recognises the place or importance of nationalism in India and, as a Marxist, come to terms with it, to do so does not even remotely mean that one identifies with it in a manner as to internalise it and make a nationalist perspective one's basic theoretical framework for understanding what is happening in our country, including the heightened importance of communalism, or to regard nationalism as the sovereign remedy for all the ills, including communalism, afflicting Indian society today.

A powerful social, political and ideological force in modern India, nationalism (including nationalist movement or politics) is yet a historical phenomenon with class and society specific character, potentialities and limitations. As such, nationalism is not something progressive, or for that matter reactionary, in itself. On the contrary, whether nationalism (or nationalist politics) is one or the other, or anything better or worse, this is determined by its specific character, its programme and leadership, and above all by the concrete historical conjuncture. Thus nationalism in India before 1947 was indeed progressive; under a different, more advanced class leadership and programme it could have been radical, even revolutionary. It was progressive because it aimed at resolving the basic structural contradiction of Indian society, congealed in imperialism, whose resolution, *against* imperialism, alone could clear the path for Indian people's continuing struggle for a better future. But nationalism need not be necessarily or entirely so in the post 1947 period. For the settlement of 1947 had its own harsh logic. It is customary in conventional scholarship or historiography to take a liberal, linear view of the historical process in India around 1947. In this view the Indian nation, or 'nation in the making' if you prefer, is seen as winning *political* freedom for India in 1947, and then, expediently and almost unproblematically, moving on to win *economic* freedom for the country—a movement which forty years hence is still on. The real historical process, however, has been quite different, essentially dialectical. The very manner in which the contradiction with imperialism was resolved, its 'transfer of power' involving no basic economic or social structural change, but putting new, now *Indian* ruling classes in control of the state power—this made the Indian people's struggle for economic freedom not only that much more complex and difficult but also primarily a matter of struggle against these classes. (Metaphorically speaking, it is not Gandhi's peasant but a Birla who inherited India in 1947. And the new rulers, subject to the necessities of the objective situation, soon set about using their newly won state power to facilitate the growth of a government-supported capitalism, while maintaining the class-exploitative-structure of the Indian society as a whole. Here the *subjective* concerns of the new rulers mattered, but marginally. Rhetoric of 'socialism' only served to deceive and win mass support. It is fashionable to laud Nehru as one who gave India 'the vision of socialism: It can be far more justifiably argued that, in effect, he reduced socialism to 'a vision' in India.) Given the new configuration of classes, class interests and contradictions, even the Indian people's continuing struggle against imperialism, or neo-colonialism of the transnationals, is no longer merely a continuation of the old anti-imperialist struggle; to be really effective, it has now to be waged as a part of this more basic struggle. For the imperialist or neo-colonialist intervention in our country today takes place, mainly though not entirely, by the grace of and through the opportunities provided by precisely the Indian ruling classes.

In this situation, nationalism or a nationalist perspective completely obscures the essential character of Indian social reality, its underlying class-exploitative economic structures whose logics is so clearly evident in the emergence of the now universally admitted 'two nations' in this country as a result of 'forty years of freedom'. Nationalism thus serves to cover up or provide alibis for the historic default or failure of the post-colonial ruling classes in India, and increasingly turns into a legitimising ideology for the new social order and the powers that be.

Scholars of the nationalist mode, wittingly or otherwise, make their own contribution to this cover-up or legitimisation. The widely used concepts of 'national economy', or 'nation-building', or 'national development', etc., each in its own way conceals the reality of an essentially capitalist development in India. (Just as the concept of 'modernisation', used by another set of scholars' does, after having served to conceal the exploitative reality of imperialism in an earlier age.) It is indeed amazing that scholars full of sensitivity for the reality of imperialist exploitation and oppression seem to lose it all when it comes to the organised structures of exploitation and oppression, old and new, that is free India's 'national economy', including Indian capitalism, even when 'progressive' or 'self reliant'!

Nationalism as an ideology in the service of the established social order is nothing new or surprising. In modern times, the ruling classes of the countries of imperialism have traditionally used nationalism to consolidate their rule at home and to defend and justify their aggression and domination abroad. More recently we have witnessed several cases of similar political-ideological use of nationalism by ruling class politicians—among these by Margaret Thatcher in England with the Falklands War, or by Ronald Reagan in the United States in his twice, successful bid for presidency. Nearer home we saw Rajiv Gandhi romp home in the unprecedented electoral triumph of 1984 on a platform of nationalism, with strong Hindu chauvinist, even anti-Sikh, overtones, and the entire opposition accused of being 'traitors'—a performance which may well be sought to be repeated whenever the next parliamentary elections are held. Marx had indeed once spoken of 'opium of patriotic feelings'. I would like to add that love for the Indian people; for India's glorious heritage through the ages, including those magnificent expressions of our people's creativity in the then inevitably religious idiom, or a *socialist* commitment to the unity and interests of the Indian people today—all this certainly does not require this opiate.

The last example in the preceding paragraph immediately points to a very common error characterising scholarly as well as 'common sense' understanding of communalism in India, which invariably regards communalism as the opposite of nationalism. This error is born of a certain facile understanding of the pre 1947 history of Indian nationalism, when it had to confront and oppose communalism as a divisive and anti-democratic force, sought to be used by imperialism to divide the Indian people and undermine their fight for freedom. Thus, it is often taken for granted that nationalism and communalism are by their very nature antithetical or mutually exclusive, that to speak up for nationalism is, *ipso facto*, to be secular and even democratic. However, this is simply not the case. This is a matter entirely of the historical conjuncture, as I have already suggested. In our times, for example, we have known nationalism of the German and Japanese varieties. With the ruling classes, in the normal pursuit of their interests or when faced with situations of crisis in the polity, nationalism has often taken all sorts of statist or racist or fascist or imperialist forms, providing ideological support or cover to the emergence of authoritarian regimes. In India today, for similar reasons, we are witnessing the Indian state, with Congress (I) in power, rapidly sliding into authoritarianism and the most important legitimising ideology is so obviously nationalism—almost hysterical in its warnings about 'the threat to the unity and integrity of India'. And what is still more relevant to my immediate argument, while the state in India is promoting or practising communalism, especially Hindu communalism, Indian nationalism is increasingly getting identified with the homogenising ideology of Hindu chauvinism. Aspirations growing out of the rich mosaic of India's diversity or plurality, especially those of its oppressed collectivities or minority groups, are viewed as so many challenges to India's 'unity and integrity' and denounced, along with all opposition to the powers that be, as 'anti-national'.

These developments draw our attention to what is possibly the most important aspect or interconnection of communalism in contemporary India, one that is usually overlooked or obscured in the nationalist perspective on the subject. The Indian ruling classes have always found religion, religiosity or *dharmikta*, as a recent coinage goes, most useful for reinforcing their hegemony, their ideological dominance and social control over the common people, making easier the latter's continued acceptance of an unjust and iniquitous social order. This usefulness has been well-secured through the typically Indian concept of secularism, defined as *sarva dharma sambhava* (equal respect for all religions). Also their political parties have never been averse to the exploitation of religion, or communalism, to a greater or lesser degree, in their struggle for power at different levels in the Indian state. But even as communalism as also religion and revivalism are there among the people and the Indian society continues to produce and reproduce these, the most significant recent development, as already noticed, is the emergence of state-sponsored or condoned communalism, religious revivalism, superstition and obscurantism, particularly the varieties associated with the majority Hindu religion, and the growing identity of Hindu chauvinist ideology with Indian nationalism. Obviously, it is here, especially in Hindu communalism or thus communalised nationalism, that the somewhat shaky Indian ruling classes are seeking, above all through their party in control of state power, the Congress (I), a newer basis of hegemony for their class rule. This heightened importance of communalism may even betoken a certain weakness of character, almost a failure of nerve on their part. For while there are problems galore, an increasing loss of credibility and even significant revolutionary developments in certain parts of the country, there is as yet no real or present threat from below to their political power or class domination. If these ruling classes, or their political representatives, are yet betraying a strong tendency to scuttle even formal secularism for communalism and religious obscurantism, or for that matter even formal democracy for an increasingly authoritarian rule, this is indicative not only of a certain degeneration at the core of the Indian political system in recent years, but also of the feudal-colonial inheritance of the new rulers of India, of a certain comprador strain inherent in the character of the dominant sections of the Indian ruling classes, including the Indian bourgeoisie as a whole.

Two final considerations regarding the nationalist perspective on communalism. The first concerns an argument which sees communalism as 'basically and above all an ideology, and declaring it to be a false one, goes on to plead for the presumably true ideology of nationalism as an effective counter to communalism. A recent definition of communalism has been going the rounds of the academy and research institutes and has been picked up and used approvingly by well-known journalists and political commentators. As a view of communalism it is much too simplistic, a good illustration indeed of the limitations of the empiricist approach to the study of communalism. Later in this note I shall be briefly commenting upon this definition and the methodology undering it. Immediately my concern is only with the argument noticed above. The definition states: 'Simply put, communalism is the belief, that because a group of people follow a particular religion, they have, as a result, common social, political and economic interests.' Elsewhere we have even more comprehensive expressions like 'common secular interests' or 'common political, economic, social and cultural interests'. We are then informed that this belief, central to communalism as an ideology, is simply false, for 'no such interests exist'. Communalism is, therefore, 'a false view...a wrong understanding of reality'. It is indeed 'a false consciousness' that comes to grip our poor, unthinking people. And salvation lies in the ideology of nationalism, 'nationalist ideology must confront and overpower communal ideology'.

Now, responding in an equally simplistic manner, one may well suggest that if we replace 'religion' with 'nation' in the above definition and recognise, as we must, not just the diversity or plurality of our people but the more basic reality of 'two nations' in India—the Indian 'twin-nation' (K N Raj), 'socio economic *dualism*' which is so very 'corrosive' (Sukhamoy Chakravarty), 'this dualism in Indian society' that is threatening to become 'explosive' (V K R V Rao)—the argument would be equally destructive of any notion of 'common political, economic, social and cultural interests' of Indians seen as belonging to a particular nation. Nationalism too would be, thus, 'a false view', 'a wrong understanding of reality', indeed 'a false consciousness'. Opposing nationalism to communalism would be a case of fighting one 'false ideology with another similarly 'false' ideology. Unless, of course, 'nationalist ideology' is *ipso facto* assumed to be true or rational, without any inadequacies, class or historical limitations, or elements of 'false consciousness'!

(This is not the place to discuss the concept of 'false consciousness' in Marxism. But increasing recourse to it in describing communalism even by scholars who know better, merits a passing, though somewhat provocative, comment.

Now, whatever the fruitfulness of this concept elsewhere (for example, in the work of Georg Lukacs); its usage in speaking of communalism as an ideological phenomenon is not particularly enlightening. Thus E P Thompson, with many others, does not consider it to be a 'happy' notion to deal with 'such ideological consciousness'. Despite this, if the concept of 'false consciousness' has caught on, it has, perhaps, less to do with its usefulness and more with the need for sophistication, especially of the Marxist sort, it lends to one's argument. This apart, once any concept is so used by an established scholar or two, 'the repute system' begins to work; and thus it is that even this rather ambiguous concept has come to acquire a life of its own in academic or journalistic writing on communalism.)

My other consideration here relates to an interesting and instructive linguistic practice in the nationalist discourse on communalism—its almost obsessive use of the term 'unfortunate'. Those, especially on the Left, who argue in the nationalist mode in their scholarship or historiography or politics, whenever they are confronted with certain unpleasant facts or practices, inadequacies or limitations, defaults or failures of Indian nationalism, nationalist politics or leadership in relation to communalism—for that matter even elsewhere as, for example, in relation to land reforms—they invariably tend to rationalise them as something 'unfortunate'. Now there may be some justification for this linguistic practice when speaking of events in the immediate present, when within the necessities of a given objective situation, politics is still a realm of possibilities, of choices to be made, and therefore the choice being made legitimately open to judgment not only on empirical or scientific grounds but on meaningful ethical or moral grounds as well. But once a particular possibility has been realised and the choices are closed, once the deed is done and it is discovered to be 'unfortunate', the real task is a historical materialist explanation of what actually came to pass. The nationalist perspective has a persistent tendency to evade this task and rest content with the moral judgment, 'unfortunate' as if this was also an adequate empirical explanation of what happened. This linguistic practice not only condones the historic defaults or failures of Indian nationalism, nationalist politics or leadership concerning communalism, but also obscures their ultimate basis in the class and history determined character of this nationalism, nationalist politics or leadership.

III

Let me now turn to the major methodological limitation of recent work on communalism, namely an empiricist approach which in its concern with 'the immediately observable *fact*', with phenomena in their appearance and isolation, fails to see their complex character and underlying interconnections with the larger social reality. Such empiricism is often ahistorical too, even when ostensibly claiming to be otherwise. A good illustration here is the argument based on the widely accepted definition of communalism which we have already noticed. The essential point of this argument is a simple assertion, in the form of a denial, which is presented as something immediately obvious or easily observed. It is denied that 'a group of people' who follow 'a particular religion' can have any 'common political, economic, social and cultural interests' because, it is asserted, 'no such interests exist'.

This argument is poor history in its understanding of communal identity as it emerges and comes to be accepted, ascribed or even imposed in real life. And it is poor sociology in its understanding of that highly complex social phenomenon, religion and, consequently, its relationship with the problem of communalism. The argument is poor history because whatever apparent plausibility its denial may have in the abstract and for secularism of the simple-minded, it has none at all at the level of concrete existential reality. For once communalism, or a similar phenomenon like racism, has emerged as a historical fact, whatever its causation, religious or racial or secular, once as a result of certain historical processes, oppression and discrimination relative to religion or race have come into being, those so oppressed and discriminated against inevitably come to acquire 'common secular interests', 'common political, economic, social and cultural interests', precisely because they belong or are seen to belong to a particular religion or race. These interests now exist as an objective, empirically verifiable fact of social life.

The Blacks in the United States, the Jews in fascist Germany, the Muslims in India are some of the obvious examples, though the extent of discrimination and oppression has varied in each case. More recently, before our very eyes, as was not the case earlier, the Sikhs are beginning to acquire a similar commonality of interests in India as a whole, as are the Hindus, in a somewhat different manner, in Punjab. At times, in India, and abroad too, that irreducible basis of all interests, secular or any other, *life* itself, comes to be at stake as the 'common interest' of a group of people defined by themselves or by others in religious or racial terms. It is indeed poor history to wish away these historically produced harsh truths of life with the facility of a simple definition and an equally simple denial!*

Poor history, the argument is equally poor sociology in its treatment of religion, an admittedly crucial factor in the

---

* In some tired moments now, even I find myself saying: 'I want to go home'. But where is 'home' in this country today? Perhaps only in the ranks of the people struggling for a just and discrimination-free society. But I no longer have the stamina for that.

making of communalism in India. This treatment is typically representative of a certain simple-minded liberal or 'rationalist' view of religion, religious beliefs or identities, or religion-related phenomena like revivalism, fundamentalism or communalism—a view which fails to give due recognition to the essential nature of religion and religious phenomena, their powerful historical presence in our country, and their complex interrelationship with what we have come to know as communalism in contemporary India.

Insofar as religion does provide a certain irreducible basis for communalism in India, and in understanding and taking care of communalism, we need to understand and take care of religion also, we must grasp its essential nature as a social-psychological phenomenon. Here, for a proper scientific or rational view, Karl Marx's fragmentary observations on religion (or criticism of religion) still remain most relevant. He wrote:

> The foundation of irreligious criticism is: *Man makes religion*, religion does not make man. Religion is indeed the self-consciousness and self-esteem of man who has either not yet won through to himself or has already lost himself again. But *man* is no abstract being squatting outside the world. Man is *the world of man*, state, society. This state and this society produce religion, which is an *inverted consciousness of the world*, because they are an *inverted world*. Religion is the general theory of this world, its encyclopaedic compendium, its logic in popular form, its spiritual *point d'honneur*, its enthusiasm, its moral sanction, its solemn complement and its universal basis of consolation and justification. It is the *fantastic realisation* of the human essence since the human essence has not acquired any true reality. The struggle against religion is therefore indirectly the struggle against that *world* whose spiritual *aroma* is religion.
>
> *Religious* suffering is at one and the same time the *expression* of real suffering and a protest against real suffering. Religion is the sigh of the oppressed creature, the heart of a heartless world and the soul of soulless conditions. It is the *opium* of the people.

> The abolition of religion as the *illusory* happiness of the people is the demand for their *real* happiness. To call on them to give up their illusions *about their condition is to call on them to give up a condition that requires illusions.* The criticism of religion is therefore in *embryo the criticism of that vale of tears* of which religion is the *halo.*
>
> Criticism has plucked the imaginary flowers of the chain not in order that man shall continue to bear that chain without fantasy or consolation but so that he shall throw off the chain and pluck the living flower. The criticism of religion disillusions man, so that he will think, act and fashion his reality like a man who has discarded his illusions and regained his senses, so that he will move around himself as his own true sun. Religion is only the illusory sun which revolves around man as long as he does not revolve around himself. It is therefore the *task of history,* once the *other world of truth* has vanished, to establish the *truth of this world.* It is the immediate *task of philosophy,* which is in the service of history, to unmask self-estrangement in its *unholy forms* once the *holy form* of human self-estrangement has been unmasked. Thus the criticism of heaven turns into the criticism of earth, the *criticism of religion* into the *criticism of law* and the *criticism of theology* into the *criticism of Politics* ....

The Most important conclusion for purposes of my argument is that criticism of religion and of the inter related phenomena of revivalism and fundamentalism, and communalism, especially as it is also an escape into or aggressive assertion of an identity based on religion, must become a criticism of the society that makes religion and the rest of them both necessary and possible.

Also, in taking care of religion, apart from understanding its essential nature, it is well to remember that religion in history often arose as the ideology and practice of powerful; progressive social movements. (Cf, Christianity, Islam, Sikhism, etc.). That, given their religious character and other class-historical limitations, these movements in due course lost their positive momentum and that religion, organised or otherwise, increasingly came to be a conservative, even reactionary factor in social life, manipulated by the ruling classes for their own ends and socialising the common people into a more or less passive acceptance of different oppressive and iniquitous social orders—all this and worse should not lead us to ignore the radical traditions or positive potentialities within religion even today—witness 'the liberation theology' in Latin America and elsewhere. Though recovery and realisation of these traditions or potentialities raises a host of difficult and delicate issues for contemporary radical or revolutionary movements, and for good historical reasons religion *as such* can no longer play its earlier progressive role, much less provide the resources, theoretical or practical, for any revolutionary reconstruction of society in our times. In any case we must not underestimate the importance of religion as a social force; it has, for good or ill, a continuing reality and rhythm of its own in our society. It persists as a significant element not only in personal identity, but even more so in the cultures of especially the so-called 'third world'. Quite often it is a crucial element in the culture of the poor and the oppressed. All this suggests the need for a sophisticated, deeper understanding of religion and related matters than is commonly available with the currently fashionable anti-communalism and secularism. A Voltairean instrumental or even genuine enlightenment rationalism, or the seemingly more modern 'scientific temper' view, happy working with its simple dichotomies of 'true' and 'false', or an abstract, essentially ahistorical attitude that mechanistically separates the religious from the secular (including even the social and the cultural) and is inclined to be cavalier or dismissive about issues of religion and religious identity, this will simply not do—however scientific or secular all this may appear to be!

The empiricist approach not only remains concerned with the apparent or the immediately observable, often with 'the abstracted almighty unimportant fact' as C Wright Mills once put it, it also means a study of phenomena in their separateness or isolation. Notwithstanding eclectic references to 'economy' or 'social basis', etc., or occasional recognition of certain interconnections, scholars have generally tended to privilege the phenomenon of communalism as such; and at times only a particular part, aspect or moment of it, for study and analysis. This has certainly yielded, as already noticed, valuable new information and insights concerning communalism in specific areas—historiography, education, media, riots or disturbances, etc. What is missed, however, are the interconnections, internal within communalism and, even more important, external with the society as a whole, 'the social ensemble' which communalism itself is a part of. The result is partial, or what Marx would have called only 'one sided' accounts of one kind or the other.

In a widely accepted view, for example, one aspect, ideology, is so privileged as to subsume virtually the whole of communalism under it. A scholar has written: 'Communalism is above all a communal ideology and it is at the level of struggle against that ideology that the way out has to be found. Any other way out will prove to be no way out at all. That will be like treating a cancer patient with aspirin because there exists a headache or stomach ache... A headache can be caused by many diseases. The real problem is that disease, not the headache or some other ache.'

In another commonly held view the focus is on 'communalism as politics'. 'The communal phenomenon', it is stated, 'is political in genesis'; it is primarily the pursuit of politics by other, that is, communal means; therefore, it is bad politics, even 'anti politics' according to one scholar. The evil of communalism thus located in politics, the solution is an appeal to all and sundry, including political parties, to eschew it and practice only non-communal or secular, 'genuine' politics.

Yet again, there is another view, particularly popular with scholars of radical persuasion. Sometimes simply economic determinist—'communalism today is the product of capitalism' etc.—more often it involves an emphasis on 'the economic factor' underlying communalism in India—slow economic *growth*, lack of employment especially for the middle or lower-middle classes, competition for scarce jobs and other economic opportunities, trade rivalry, etc. or we are offered a theory of 'macro as well as micro factors', and 'among the macro factors are country-wide socio economic changes'. This view too has its truth like the earlier ones. One may even concede that 'economics of communalism' has an importance' all its own. Yet as 'a theory of factors', the economic version, this view too remains within the empiricist framework. And so on.

At other times, not one aspect or another but communalism as such is so privileged and all sense of other parts or interconnections of the social whole lost, that it comes to be seen, with its dangerous divisive distortions, as a source of almost every other problem in sight. Communalism may even come to be offered as a simple, straightforward explanation of some of the most complex historical developments. Thus, apropos Punjab it has been argued: 'it is communalism which has led to separatism and then to terrorism'—without any reference to the structural interconnections of these phenomena, *via* mediations, with the historically specific but essentially capitalist economic development of India (including the green revolution) or, at another level, with the politics practised by the ruling classes in India and in this state in recent years or, at yet another level, with the host of complex historically produced factors in Punjab itself that have gone into the making of the tragedy that is Punjab today—and so on. Communalism virtually swamps everything, all other issues in the situation including the far more basic ones, and people's struggle there is reduced to a struggle against communalism, particularly Sikh communalism. It is as simple as: 'nation' versus 'communalism, separatism and terrorism'. There cannot be a better example of 'barefoot empiricism' at work in the study of communalism in modern India.

Scholarship in the empiricist mode has certainly gained for us a great deal of 'retail sanity' about communalism in contemporary India. But because of its inherent limitations, it fails to see the 'whole-sale madness' which has today come to characterise the Indian society as a whole—its economy, politics, ideology, culture and so on—in which communalism, an 'insanity' itself, has become functional at the present historical conjuncture.

IV

As Marxism views it, society is not merely an aggregate or random togetherness of parts, factors, levels or instances. It is a social whole, or totality, a historically specific structured interdependence of parts, with an economic structural base and loaded with contradictions that account for its dynamics, its concrete *over-determined* historical development. In other words, this determination, insofar as we must use this term, is neither unique, nor is it to be understood in any economic or class reductionist manner; it is something far more complex and problematic, realised on an economic base, but through any number of interactions and mediations. The important point is that the parts, aspects or instances, generally referred to as super structure, along with their contradictions, are not some epiphenomenal manifestations of the economic base. On the contrary, they may and often do have an autonomous, irreducible, historically specific existence of their own. But this is an existence of dialectical, determined and determining relationships to each other and to the social whole. And the dynamics of this existence, the working out of their contradictions, is most decisively *conditioned* by the basic economic contradictions, the structural logic of the economic base. One might add that it is only within the necessities and constraints of the given objective, economic-structural situation, within this 'determination by the economic in the *first* instance', that whatever happens, every complex historical effect or outcome is *ultimately* determined by the activity of men in pursuit of their needs or puposes.

Viewed thus, from a Marxist perspective, different parts or problems of Indian society with all their conflicts and contradictions relating to religion or politics, caste, language or religion, ethnicity or nationality, ideology or culture, women's oppression or national integration, etc. do not exist totally apart from each other or from society, the social whole. And while these often do have a historically specific autonomous reality of their own, their dynamics is decisively conditioned by the economic structural logic of the continental social formation that is India today. And this is the logic of a development, which is essentially capitalist in nature; though it has a historically specific character of its own which scholars variously refer to when they speak of a state or government-supported capitalism, weak or retarded or backward capitalism, underdeveloped capitalism or capitalist under-development or even 'peripheral' or 'compradore-bureaucratic' capitalism, etc. It is in this sense alone that the problems or conflicts mentioned above, including those relating to religion or communalism, are economy or class dependent. A class perspective today has to accommodate the rich diversity of contemporary Indian social reality even as it lays emphasis on the crucial importance of the economic base and its structural logic that conditions the dynamics of this diversity. Needless to add, without such emphasis Marxism would be theoretically indistinguishable from any other 'sociology'. And it is not without reason that today, especially in the absence of class-based people's politics, all the identities, all the divides and fissures of Indian society are simultaneously becoming significant and explosive. This is equally true of the explosive emergence of communalism in recent years.

It is important to recognise that communalism is in a sense a false ideology (even if the concept of 'false consciousness' is not very helpful); or that it is a corruption of even bourgeois-democratic politics (which in a way it is); or that economic factors significantly contribute to the rise and spread of communalism (which they indeed do); or that communalism is a 'modern' phenomenon (which perhaps could be said of just about everything today barring odd 'historical substrata')... All this, the 'truths' so discovered, is certainly important and therein lies the value of the work done in the empiricist mode. But we must seek an understanding of communalism, which including all this and more is a totalising, all-sided understanding which, even as it grasps communalism's specific aspects or autonomous reality and its certain irreducible basis in religion, seeks to explore the entire ensemble of its social interconnections—above all with economy but also with history and politics and ideology and culture, etc.—especially those which have made it the explosive issue it is in Indian society today. More of these interconnections we are able to grasp, more true and therefore more effective politically will be our understanding of communalism in contemporary India.

Illustratively, but only so, such an understanding at the basic economic level must take notice of Indian society, with its long history and massive feudal-colonial inheritance, undergoing, as V K R V Rao has put it: 'a type of capitalist development in the interest of a narrow section of Indian society'. In an effort to grasp something of the historical specificity of 'our national economy', Romesh Thapar once described it as 'some strange kind of corrupted capitalist growth'. It may be relevant here to recall what Marx once wrote, of course in a different historical context. He spoke of countries which 'suffer not only from the development of capitalist production, but also from the incompleteness of that development. Alongside of modern evils, a whole series of inherited evils oppress us, arising from the passive survival of antequated modes of production with their inevitable train of social and political anachronisms. We suffer not only from the living but from the dead.' Indian economic development with its structural logic of inequality and unevenness has produced not only 'two India' and an ever widening gulf between the two with all its disintegrative consequences, but also, together with poverty and hunger and heart-breaking inhuman conditions of life for the vast masses of our people, a society of myriad old and new oppressions, insecurities and alienations, with no jobs or ideals for its youth or vision and values for the people, a society in deep social and moral crisis indeed—thus providing a continuing social-material basis for the production and reproduction, sustenance and reinforcement of all sorts of religiosity or *dharmikta*, revivalism, fundamentalism and obscurantism, and also ideologies and practices like communalism. (Apropos 'the Punjab problem', for example, it is well to remember that the green revolution, as an integral part of Indian capitalist development, has meant not only 'economic growth' but also sharpened economic disparities, class divisions and social tensions. And in its progress it turned Punjab into 'a chicken-and- whisky-land', giving rise to an extraordinary corruption and vulgarity of life and culture in the state. This, in the absence of strong countervailing democratic or socialist culture, should explain a great deal about the compensatory appeal of religious fundamentalism, with its harking back to the puritanical traditions of early Sikhism, etc.)

At another level, our understanding must also take notice of the politics of the ruling classes spawned by Indian economic development, presided over by a bourgeoisie born old without ever having known youth, with none of the possible virtues of youth and all the vices of old age. This politics as recently practised by their political formations—well-described as 'Hindu Undivided Family'—especially by the dominant Congress (I), has not only turned politics itself into a highly capital-intensive business, but with its totally unscrupulous, no-holds-barred quality and the accompanying corruption, criminalisation and lumpenisation, also become a potent threat to India's always weak and fragile democracy and an increasingly deadly exercise for the Indian people. Here it is truly the end justifying the means—any means including the use of every form of religious revivalism, fundamentalism and obscurantism, and, of course, communalism.

In a similar manner we need to explore communalism's interconnections in the realms of ideology and culture and other important domains of contemporary Indian society, all bearing the signature of the whole; above all, of its corrupt and corrupting capitalist socio economic development. Our understanding must also take account of the specificities of particular situations, community and region-wise, the entire wealth of 'little truths' or 'micro factors' that competent empirical studies have revealed. But in the immediate historical context the most significant fact to be recognised is that the heightening of communalism today is simultaneously the product of social, moral and political crisis in society and the reaction of the ruling classes to this crisis. With the older basis of their power and hegemony weakening, they are increasingly turning to communalism in general and to Hindu communalism in particular, to win votes, fragment and divide the people and, above all, secure their continued political and ideological dominance over them. Faced with a worsening economic situation for the people and mounting discontent, widespread violence, disruption and disorder in civil society, and their deepest-ever crisis of legitimacy since independence, the ruling classes, through their dominant political formation, the

Congress (I), are seeking increasingly authoritarian, even fascist answers to their problems. It is in this overall context, essentially a context of classes and class struggle, open or hidden, actual or potential, that communalism as ideology and practice has become functional, more than ever before, in contemporary India.

Such would be the thrust of a Marxist study or understanding of communalism today as against the empiricist study or understanding. Study of communalism in the empiricist mode, outside of its social structural context and historical conjuncture, besides resulting in partial or 'one sided' accounts, has in fact another significant negative consequence. The empiricist privileging of communalism as such and, therefore, of the conflicts and oppositions it apparently expresses, may prevent recognition of the more objective socio economic divisions and oppositions of interests in Indian society. In other words, the contradictions that communalism immediately represents may come to obscure or conceal the more basic structural or class contradictions of Indian society, obscuring or concealing them by their displacement. This can only disorient and emasculate the political practice of the exploited and the oppressed in our country. For they need to articulate their struggle against communalism with their more basic class struggles. Just as the related struggles of our oppressed and discriminated-against minority groups or identifies, religious as well as others, including women, dalits and tribals, for their human and democratic rights, have also to be so articulated, in theory and practice, with a class based people's politics, if they are not to distort or corrupt their consciousness still further, divide the oppressed even more, and end up only serving the exploiting elements or other vested interests within these minorities or identities.

V

One last point before I conclude with a tentative definition of communalism in contemporary India. This point is relevant to the ongoing theorising on communalism but even more so to the struggle against it. It also needs to be made in the context of somewhat undermined yet continuing myth of 'value free' social analysis. It is a myth because by its very nature truth in social sciences, concerned as they are with our class divided societies, is partisan, at times even political dynamite, unlike truth in natural sciences which is by and large politically neutral. The discovery of truth here, if difficult because of the specific nature of its subject matter, is very risky and dangerous also, which partly accounts for the general backwardness of the social sciences. No wonder we have Kant's injunction: 'Dare to know!' And Marx in an early passage, which may well serve as a motto for any worthwhile social science scholarship, wrote: 'Our task is ruthless criticism of everything that exists, ruthless in the sense that the criticism will not shrink either from its own conclusions or from conflict with the powers that be.' Immediately, however, I am interested in making a slightly different but more pertinent point, namely, in social analysis explanation and prescription invariably go together, just as a diagnosis always points to the treatment. As a matter of fact in any concrete human activity, whose characteristic is *purpose*, knowing and doing are always interconnected—such is the dialectics of facts and values in real life. In other words, an explanation or understanding of any social reality always has a 'value slope'. This, I want to suggest, is true of every understanding or explanation of communalism in contemporary India.

Thus if you understand communalism empiricistically, focussing either on one of its aspects, or on it as such but in isolation from its interconnections as a part of the social whole—at which level alone an effective solution of the problems it presents is possible—you will seek, at best, only *liberal*, partial or reformist, answers, or at worst, indulge in moral rhetoric or ideological posturing, generally of the nationalist variety. For example, if you understand communalism as 'basically and above all' an ideology, then inevitably 'it is at the level of struggle against that ideology that the way out has to be found. Any other way out will prove to be no way out at all'. The prescription or the 'value slope' indicated is a struggle at the level of ideas alone—'all out mass ideological campaign', scholarly critiques or exposures, non communal education or historiography, cultivation of 'scientific temper' and of course the advocacy of the ideologies of nationalism, secularism, 'true religion' and so on. Any other 'level of struggle' is ruled out, certainly the struggle in the more basic areas of economy or politics, more specifically, the economy and politics of the ruling classes and the ideology and culture spawned by these. Incidentally, this understanding makes it easily possible, often comfortable and rewarding too, for scholars of diverse sorts, including 'leftists', even 'Marxists', to line up behind the Indian ruling classes and their political representatives in the name of fighting against communalism.

If your understanding is based on some awareness of the structured nature of social reality and, therefore, recognises at least some important interconnections of communalism, but not the economic structural ones, that mediate the phenomenon of communalism with the social whole that is Indian society, then the prescription that follows will involve somewhat *radical* answers to the problem of communalism. For example, those who see the role of the 'economic factor' in the situation seek to combine, at least in theory, the ideological struggle with an assertive advocacy of 'economic growth', 'radical economic changes', 'provision of more jobs' or 'better economic opportunities' and so on.

If, however, your understanding of communalism is aware of its basic structural interconnections also, if it recognises the economic basis of Indian society that decisively conditions the dynamics of communalism in the interrelated areas of personal life, politics, ideology, culture, etc., the prescription will be a struggle against communalism from a *revolutionary* standpoint which, even as it values and includes the struggles of the liberal and the radical, sees this struggle as a part of the Indian people's broader struggle against the ruling *classes*, against their economy, politics, ideology, culture, etc., a struggle *against* the present economic and social order and *for* socialism. Such a strategic revolutionary perspective does indeed require extraordinary resilience of tactics. But it is not a question of 'against communalism' versus 'for socialism' as has been suggested in some crude, typically empiricist, theoretical formulations on the subject; here is an example: 'As a Marxist, I do not believe that communalism will not end till socialism comes and therefore believers in socialism should not fight against communalism, but fight only for socialism'. Or it is mistakenly argued that the first and immediate task is to somehow hold the country together against communalism and other divisive or disintegrative developments so that later, one day, we may build socialism in it! On the contrary, the struggle against communalism and the struggle for socialism must not be seen as two separate struggles, it is not at all a question of either/or, before and after, now and later. The struggle against communalism and for secularism in India today has to be understood and waged as a part of the overall revolutionary struggle for socialism in India. In the Marxist perspective, insofar as communalism and secularism are indeed among the more significant issues facing the Indian people, the struggle against communalism has to be a struggle against more than communalism, just as a struggle for secularism has to be a struggle for more than only secularism in India.

VI

Finally, the definition and a footnote. Conventional academic scholarship has always had a certain fascination for definitions. May be for reasons of pedagogy and the examinations that go with it. It could also be that the empiricist mode naturally tends to abridge or congeal social reality into a lexicographical formula, a definition. So with academic scholarship on communalism. Scholars have found it necessary to begin or end their study of communalism with an attempt at defining it. Let me too, then, conclude this rather fragmentary note with a tentative definition of communalism, however alien it may be to the Marxian method of social analysis. Marx had argued that to abstract a social or economic phenomenon, for example, 'property', from its 'specific social relationships' and then define it as if it were 'an independent relation, a category apart, an abstract and eternal idea can be nothing but an illusion of metaphysics or jurisprudence'. Engels had warned against looking for 'fixed and universally applicable definitions' in Marx's work. He had, on his part, insisted that defining or conceptualisation must not involve a freezing of social phenomenon into a static formula. He wrote: 'It is a matter of course that, where things and their mutual interrelations are conceived not as fixed but as changing, their mental images, the ideas concerning them are likewise subject to change and transformation; that they cannot be sealed up in rigid definitions, but, must be developed in the historical and logical process of their formation.'

Thus in an important sense all definitions are deficient or inadequate and from a strictly scientific standpoint of rather limited value. A definition takes on a concrete meaning only when flushed or filled up with the specific social relations that constitute the reality of a phenomenon in a given social order. Yet, subject to these considerations, definitions can be convenient or useful, at times even indispensable, as the way to begin, as a guide to social analysis. A good definition will of course point to the most common, the simplest or essential in a phenomenon. But it should also be suggestive of the complex socio-historical relationships that go into the making of its concrete reality as a part of the social whole—thereby providing a point of entry into a study of this social whole as well, with its underlying structural necessities or determinations. In other words, a definition of communalism even as it points to its essential character and indicates the important social relations that go to constitute its contemporary reality, should do so in a manner that understanding communalism is also suggestive of an entry into understanding of contemporary Indian society viewed, in this case, from the vantage point of communalism.

In the light of the scattered argument of this note so far, here is a tentative definition of communalism today:

> Communalism in contemporary India, as ideology and practice, is above all an aspect of the politics of the ruling classes in a society with a massive feudal-colonial inheritance, deep religious divisions and undergoing its own historically specific form of capitalist development.

One may add that the spread or heightening of communalism and related phenomena like religious revivalism, fundamentalism, or obscurantism, is in direct proportion to the depth of the crisis in Indian polity and politics of the ruling classes on the one hand and in inverse proportion to the presence or power of the left or class-based politics of the people on the other.

Further, it can be legitimately argued that at the present historical conjuncture, given the balance of forces in our society in general and in ruling class politics in particular, if communalism ever comes to contribute to the rise of the specifically Indian form of fascist authoritarianism, the danger lies in the Congress (I), the major political formation of the Indian ruling classes and *the* party of Indian nationalism, in its quest for power, condoning or encouraging, conniving or colluding with, even succumbing to or opting for communalism in general and Hindu communalism in particular, the latter easily assuming the form of Hinduised nationalism; the parties of avowed communalism in India, traditional or new, Hindu and other, can only facilitate the process.

Such a denouement of ruling class politics in India would indeed be a tragedy for the Indian people—the worst in a long list so far. It needs to be opposed and fought against by all means and at all costs. It can and must be averted.

But the beginning of wisdom and the possibility of a successful fight here lies in recognising that, especially in recent years, the ruling class politics, while preserving the organised structures of exploitation and oppression in India, has been producing only tragedies for the Indian people. It is time we are 'nationalist' or 'patriotic' enough to have more faith in our own ruling classes. Today they are fully self-reliant, they can produce all the tragedies they need for the Indian people, by themselves. They don't have to depend upon imperialism, etc. not for this in any case.

The footnote. There are among us a very large number of honest and well-meaning people—from the nationalist politics, no longer as justified historically as it once was, or in nationalist scholarship, which was and is intellectually always suspect—who for reasons of understanding or compulsions of age, experience or habits of thought, are incapable of thinking in any but the nationalist mode. They would do well to remember that perceptive scholars of the situation in post-colonial societies of the third world have spoken of 'anti-nation within the nation', and this is true not in the generally intended or understood narrow economic sense only. And if such persons would yet define the historic task of the Indian people in nationalist terms, today it can be nothing other than rescuing the 'nation' from its ruling classes.

Chapter 3

Communalism in Contemporary India*

Some Theoretical Considerations

Communalism was a major social and political problem in our country during the colonial period; it gained yet another basis and lease of life with the partitioned independence of 1947, and has acquired a truly explosive dimension in recent years. It is significant that while there is general abhorrence of communalism and literally none in this country would like to be described or known as a communalist, communalism persists, an ugly presence in our everyday life and a potent threat to the life and property of our people in large parts of the country and to their struggle for a better life everywhere. The need to understand communalism, and to struggle against it, was never more imperative than it is today. What follows is a modest effort in this regard, based on what I have already written on the subject elsewhere.**

One aspect of the matter needs to be immediately taken note of. We must recognise that, once arisen, like any other

---

* Public Lecture at Indian Social Science Congress, Berhampur, Orissa, December, 1990.

** E.g., 'Communalism and the Struggle against Communalism: A Marxist View', *Social Scientist*, Vol. 18, Nos. 8-9, August-September 1990.

socially significant phenomenon, communalism has come to acquire an autonomous reality and logic of its own. As such, subject of course to the ebb and flow of the country's social and political life, especially the shifts within bourgeois politics, communalism today has an extraordinary diversity of forms or aspects, community, region or economy-wise peculiarities and variations, complex and changing historical contexts or conjunctures, and a certain specificity of expression each time, including riots or its use by the different political formations of the ruling classes at different times, occasionally even in their factional infighting, and so on. These are indeed among considerations of great tactical importance in the struggle against communalism, for there is no escaping *the absolute necessity* of fighting communalism in each and every one of its expressions on its own specific terrain. This is an essential part of any effective struggle against communalism. And it is in this area that competent scholarly work on communalism has made its most valuable contribution.

My concern in this lecture, however, in not with these specificities of communalism but with a few issues of general nature, clarity regarding which, I believe, may help towards a better, more true, and therefore politically more effective understanding of communalism in contemporary India (including its reality and logic as an autonomous phenomenon).

The first issue concerns the decisive importance of *how* you understand or explain contemporary communalism, for this determines how you will proceed to struggle against it, what will be the focus or main thrust of this struggle. In social scientific thinking much has been made in recent years of the *logical* disjunction between facts and values, between explanation and prescription, and there has been an ignorant, philosophically illiterate insistence upon 'value freedom' or 'ethical neutrality' in social science scholarship. This is not the place or occasion to discuss this problem. Nor is it necessary. For my argument it is enough to recognise and counter insist that in all human activity, whose characteristic is *purpose*, knowing and doing are so related that explanation is invariably suggestive of prescription, just as a diagnosis always points to the treatment. In other words, an explanation or understanding of any social phenomenon, always has a 'value slope'. And this, I suggest, is true of every understanding or explanation of communalism in contemporary India.

Thus, if 'religion' is central to your understanding of communalism, the remedy will necessarily lie in exhortations on behalf of either 'true religion' or, from the other end, cultivation and spread of 'scientific temper'. An explicitly formulated variant of this kind of understanding, which infact has emerged as the most widely accepted theory today is the view that 'communalism is above all a communal ideology', a dangerously 'false' ideology. That being the case, it only follows that 'it is at the level of struggle against that ideology that the way out has to found. Any other way out will prove to be no way out at all.' The 'value slope' indicated is a struggle at the level of ideas alone—any other 'level of struggle' is simply explained out. (Incidentally, those who understand and argue in this manner generally hold that salvation lies in the ideology of nationalism: 'nationalist ideology must confront and overpower communal ideology'). Again, if the evil of communalism is primarily located in politics as such, the solution almost inevitably turns out to be an appeal to all and sundry, including political parties, to eschew such 'pseudo-politics' or 'anti-politics' as scholars have called it, and practice non-communal or secular, some kind of 'true' or 'genuine' politics. Or, if you go by an 'economic interpretation' of communalism, the prescription will be a demand for 'rapid economic development', 'more job opportunities', etc. And so on.

Such explanations, each in its own partial manner, certainly partake of the truth about communalism in contemporary India and the forms of active intervention suggested by these explanations are indeed important in any struggle against communalism today. But 'the truth is the whole' as Hegel put it. And if therefore we have an understanding of communalism which, including all this and more, is a totalising, all-sided understanding, which even as it recognises communalism's specific aspects or autonomous reality and its certain irreducible basis in religion or religious identity, seeks to grasp the entire ensemble of its social interconnections, above all with economy but also with history and politics, ideology and culture, etc., especially those which have made it the explosive issue it is in Indian society today, the prescription will be: a really effective struggle against communalism has to be a *revolutionary* struggle, which even as it values and includes within itself every form of particular intervention or struggle against communalism, is a part of the Indian people's larger struggle for a better life, for a sane and just, a genuinely secular and democratic society that guarantees a life of dignity and honour to all its citizens.

The second issue concerns what is possibly the most common ideological error characterising scholarly as well as 'common sense' understanding of communalism in India, which invariably regards communalism as the opposite of nationalism. Nationalism is, by definition as it were, assumed to be secular, a view typically expressed in the daily invocatory reference by anyone and everyone these days to 'national and secular forces' in India. This error is born of a certain facile understanding of the pre-1947 history of Indian nationalism and is reinforced by an equally facile understanding of what happened in India when it gained its independence in 1947.

Indian nationalism had to confront and oppose communalism as a divisive and anti democratic force, sought to be used by imperialism to divide the Indian people and undermine their fight for freedom. Thus, it is often taken for granted that nationalism and communalism are by their very nature antithetical or mutually exclusive, that to speak up for nationalism is, *ipso facto*, to be secular, and even democratic. However, this is simply not the case. A certain historical justification for this view notwithstanding, even for the pre-1947 period it is today well to recognise that Gandhi and bourgeois-led Indian nationalism, along with its other limitations, carried a great deal of Hindu and other communal baggage with it, and that its 'final triumph' in 1947 was at the same time a compromise and settlement with imperialism which partitioned the country along communal lines, with disastrous long-term consequences for the common people on both sides of the borders.

As regards what happened in 1947, its essential character, we need to recognise that a powerful social, political and ideological force in modern India, nationalism (including nationalist movement or politics) is yet a historical phenomenon with class and society-specific character, potentialities and limitations, and usefulness too. As such, nationalism is not something progressive or for that matter reactionary in itself. On the contrary, whether nationalism (or nationalist politics) is one or the other, or anything better or worse, this is determined by its specific character, its programme and leadership, and above all by the concrete historical conjuncture. Thus nationalism in India before 1941 was indeed progressive; under a different, more advanced class leadership and programme, it could have been radical, even revolutionary. It was progressive because it aimed at resolving the basic structural contradictions of Indian society, congealed in imperialism, whose resolution, *against* imperialism, alone could clear the path for the Indian people's continuing struggle for a better future. But nationalism need not be necessarily or entirely so in the post-1947 period. For the settlement of 1947 had its own harsh logic. It is customary in conventional scholarship or historiography to take a liberal, linear view of the historical process in India around 1947. In this view the Indian nation, or 'nation-in-the-making' if you prefer, is seen as winning *political* freedom for India in 1947 and then expectedly and almost unproblematically moving on to win *economic* freedom for the country—a movement which forty-three years hence is still on. The real historical process, however, has been quite different, essentially dialectical. The very manner in which the contradiction with imperialism was resolved, its 'transfer of power' involving no basic economic or social structural change, but putting new, now *Indian* ruling classes in control of the state power, this made the Indian people's struggle for economic freedom not only that much more complex and difficult but alto primarily a matter of struggle against these classes. For the same reason, even the Indian people's continuing fight against imperialism, or neo- colonialism of the transnationals, is no longer simply a continuation of the old anti-imperialist fight; henceforth it too can be effectively waged only as a part of this more basic struggle. For the imperialist intervention or domination in our country now takes place primarily by the grace of and through the opportunities provided by precisely the new rulers of India.

For my present argument the point to be noticed is that the Indian ruling classes have, over the years, used their state power to facilitate a kind of socio-economic development in India which has led to the emergence in this country of the now universally admitted 'two nations'—the Indian 'twin-nation' (K N Raj), 'socio-economic *dualism*' which is so very 'corrosive' (Sukhamoy Chakravarty), 'this dualism in Indian society' that is threatening to become 'explosive' (V K R V Rao), the 'two Indias' of Rajni Kothari, V P Singh,

R K Hegde *et al*, etc. In this situation nationalism or nationalist perspective only obscures the essential character of Indian social reality today, its underlying exploitative and oppressive socio-economic structures, and thus serves to cover up or provide alibis for the historic default of the post-colonial ruling classes in India, and increasingly turns into a legitimising ideology for the new social order and the powers that be.

Nationalism as an ideology in the service of the established social order is nothing new or surprising. In modem times, the ruling classes of the countries of imperialism have traditionally used nationalism to consolidate their rule at home and to defend and justify their aggression and domination abroad. More recently we have witnessed several cases of similar political-ideological use of nationalism by ruling class politicians—among these by Margaret Thatcher in England with the Falklands War, or by Ronald Reagan in the US in his twice successful bid for the American Presidency. Nearer home we saw Rajiv Gandhi romp home in the unprecedented electoral triumph of 1984 on a platform of nationalism, with strong Hindu chauvinist, even anti-Sikh, overtones, the emerging platform of Hinduised Indian nationalism, which has now been well and properly appropriated by another political formation of the Indian ruling classes, the Bharatiya Janata Party.

Besides, we must not forget that we have known nationalism of German, Japanese and Italian varieties. With the ruling classes in the normal pursuit of their interests or when faced with situations of crisis in the polity, nationalism has often taken all sorts of statist or racist or fascist or imperialist forms, providing ideological support or cover to the emergence of reactionary authoritarian regimes. And far too often in our times people have been sacrificed to 'the nation', as has already begun to happen, in its own way, in this country too. One has only to listen to our rulers' rhetoric about 'unity and integrity of the nation' and look at their practice on the ground!

Thus in the Indian context today, a struggle against communalism from the standpoint of nationalism is, if not entirely misleading, highly inadequate and problematic. It is certainly not going to be effective unless it is at the same time a part of the struggle 'to rescue the nation' from its ruling classes, if I may put it that way.

The third issue concerns religion and religious identity which do provide a certain irreducible basis for communalism in India, and in understanding and taking care of communalism, we need to understand and take care of religion and the problems of religious identity also. Religion as such is not my concern at the moment. Here it is only necessary to reiterate the need for a critical but sophisticated treatment of the question of religion insofar as it feeds or is manipulated to feed communalism. To this I shall add a specific argument on the question of religious identity.

Discussion or treatment of religion in our country is generally much too simplistic and cliche-ridden, even in its more sublime metaphysical or philosophically esoteric passages; typically there is its idealisation and defence as simply a spiritual phenomenon that caters to our ultimate values and aspirations, or, far less often, its criticism and rejection as simply an erroneous view of things that is waiting to yield to a rational or scientific understanding, and almost always a shared ahistorical approach, a substantive denial of any *genuine* basis for religion in social reality. What is needed is a radically different, deeper understanding which, aware of the origins of religion and religious phenomena in the realm of the secular, and their continuing *social* basis, gives due recognition, at one level, to their essential socio-psychological nature and, at another, to their complex and powerful historical presence in human affairs, in India as elsewhere. Here Karl Marx's fragmentary observations on religion (or criticism of religion) still remain most relevant. He wrote:

> The foundation of irreligious criticism is: *Man makes religion*, religion does not make man. Religion is indeed the self-consciousness and self-esteem of man who has either not yet won through to himself or has already lost himself again. But *man* is no abstract being squatting outside the world. Man is *the world of man*, state, society. This state and this society produce religion, which is an *inverted consciousness of the world*, because they are an *inverted world*. Religion is the general theory of this world, its encyclopedic compendium, its logic in popular form, its spiritual *point d'honneur*, its enthusiasm, its moral sanction, its solemn complement and its universal basis of consolation and justification. It is the *fantastic realisation* of the human essence since the human essence has not acquired any true reality. The struggle against religion is therefore indirectly the struggle against *that world* whose spiritual *aroma* is religion.
>
> *Religious* suffering is at one and the same time the *expression* of real suffering and a protest against real suffering. Religion is the sigh of the oppressed creature, the heart of a heartless world and the soul of soulless conditions. It is the *opium* of the people.
>
> The abolition of religion as the *illusory* happiness of the people is the demand for their *real* happiness. To call on them to give up their illusions about their condition is to *call on them to give up a condition that requires illusions*. The criticism of religion is therefore in *embryo the criticism of that vale of tears* of which religion is the *halo*.
>
> Criticism has plucked the imaginary flowers on the chain not in order that man shall continue to bear that chain without fantasy or consolation but so that he shall throw off the chain and pluck the living flower. The criticism of religion disillusions man, so that he will think, act and fashion his reality like a man who has discarded his illusions and regained his senses, so that he will move around himself as his own true sun. Religion is only the illusory sun which revolves around man as long as he does not revolve around himself.
>
> It is therefore the *task of history*, once the *other-world of truth*

> has vanished, to establish the *truth of this world*. It is the immediate *task of philosophy*, which is in the service of history, to unmask self-estrangement in its *unholy forms* once the *holy form* of human self-estrangement has been unmasked. Thus the criticism of heaven turns into the criticism of earth, the *criticism of religion* into the *criticism of law and the criticism of theology* into *the criticism of politics*...

The most important conclusion for purposes of my argument is that the criticism of religion and the inter-related phenomena of religious revivalism and fundamentalism, and of communalism, especially as it is also an escape into, or aggressive assertion of, an identity based on religion, must become the criticism of society that makes religion and the rest of them both necessary and possible.

We also need to recognise that in the history of humankind religion often arose as the ideology and practice of powerful progressive social movements (Buddhism, Christianity, Islam, Sikhism, etc.) That, given their religious character and other class-historical limitations, these movements in due course lost their positive momentum and that religion, organised or otherwise, increasingly comes to be a conservative, even reactionary factor in social life, manipulated by the ruling classes for their own ends, above all for socialising the common people into a more or less passive acceptance of different oppressive and iniquitous social orders—all this and worse should not lead us to ignore the radical traditions or positive potentialities within religion even today; witness, for example, 'the liberation theology' in Latin America and elsewhere. Though, one must add, the recovery and realisation of these traditions or potentialities raises a host of difficult and delicate issues for contemporary radical or revolutionary people's movements, and for good historical reasons religion as such can no longer play its earlier progressive role, much less provide the basic resources, theoretical or practical, for any revolutionary reconstruction of society in our times—it can at best only help.

Be that as it may, we must not underestimate the importance of religion as a social force; it has, for good or ill, a continuing reality and rhythm of its own in our society. It persists as a significant element not only in personal identity, but even more so in the cultures of especially the so-called 'Third World'. Quite often it is a crucial element in the culture of the poor and the oppressed. All this suggests the need for a sophisticated, deeper understanding of religion and related matters than is commonly available with the currently fashionable anti communalism and secularism. A Voltairean instrumental or even genuine enlightenment rationalism, or the seemingly more modern 'scientific temper' view, happy working with its simple dichotomies of 'true' and 'false', or an abstract, essentially ahistorical attitude that mechanistically separates the religious from the secular (including even the social and the cultural) and is inclined to be cavalier or dismissive about issues of religion and religious identity, this will simply not do—however scientific or secular all this may appear to be!

Insofar as religion is an issue, it is this critical but sympathetic and sophisticated understanding of religion which should inform our struggle for secularism in India. It is a long haul, but there is no other choice. In this, as in so many other things, we must have faith in our people's interest and ability to understand. Tactical resilience is necessary but populist cliche-ridden pragmatism will not do any longer. An almost opportunist evasion of real and difficult issues here has already proved disastrous for our people.

I am not here concerned with the problems arising out of the characteristic diversity or plurality of India's extraordinarily rich social and cultural life, or with the emerging, highly visible and valid struggles of the long oppressed and more disadvantaged sections of the Indian people, 'identities' as they have come to be called: minor nationalities or ethnic groups, religious minorities, dalits, tribals, women, and so on, all impelled to action by an iniquitous economic development, all struggling against an oppressive, homogenising Indian state and India's equally oppressive social structures, and all of them seeking their rights and a place of dignity and honour among the Indian people—a development that drawing attention to the multiform social oppressions prevalent in our society, as against the conventional focus on the economic oppression, has given rise to a virtual 'identitarianism' which is such a significant but problematic feature of contemporary social scientific concerns as well as social activism. I am only interested in making a brief comment on the question of religious identity.

There is no denying the importance or value of religious identity as a form of community, for the sense of belonging it gives to its members, the social, cultural and psychological support it provides, especially in times of personal stress and social crisis. Man is indeed a social being—and this is not to be understood in the vulgar bourgeois manner but in the profound sense in which Plato argued for it against the Sophists, or, in our times, Marx asserted it as a principle of materialist humanism against bourgeois individualism. Man reaches his humanity and continues to be, ever more human, as a cooperative, communitarian being—each 'I' is, as Marx said, 'an intermediary between you and human species'. Community is inside man, just as man is inside community. His very individuality is acquired by man from community, 'his life is an expression and confirmation of social life'. Before there is a man, there are men. Or as Marx put it:

> Since he comes into the world neither with a looking glass in his hand, nor as a Fichtean philosopher, to whom 'I am 1' is sufficient, man first sees and recognises himself in other men...

The bond this recognition reflects is not something metaphysical or spiritual or even, in the first instance, psychological. It is practical—based on the need to be, to live and to survive. From community human beings receive the atmosphere and sustenance for their short flight on this earth, and through it alone they have an opportunity for whatever immortality is genuinely possible for them. Community, thus, is a positive value. And this is very true of a religious community as an identity, that is, as a historically-constituted 'recognition' of cooperation and fellowship with other human beings.

But it needs to be immediately added that the range of this 'recognition' is neither pre-given nor frozen or exclusive at a particular point of time. On the contrary, it is always, as already suggested, a historical outcome. A family or tribe, caste or class, religion or nation, or even gender—it may, one day, well come to encompass, not rhetorically, but in a meaningful sense, the entire humankind in an enriching lap over the invariably overlapping primary or intermediate identities we now have. In the meantime, however, it is well to recognise that precisely because these identities are historically constituted, they carry a whole load of history's burdensome baggage also, the mud of their times as it were —they have their negative features. A religious identity is no exception—a good example is the status and treatment of women in virtually all religious identities. In other words, an identity *as such* is not something good or sacred, a value in itself—its real life situation may have all kinds of ugly features *within* that limit or diminish human beings, struggle against which has to be a part of the larger struggle *without* for a more just and democratic social order. A concern for the rights and interests of identities does not mean condoning or perpetuation of these negative or ugly features: their own injustices, discrimination and denial of rights, inequalities or class divisions, superstitions or otherwise oppressive social practices and, almost invariably, a vision which is a barrier to seeing things the way they really are, etc. etc. Democratisation within is in fact necessary if the democratic rights struggle without is to be really effective in the interests of the identity concerned as well as the requisite democratic advance in society, and not remain only an ineffectual holding operation that simultaneously strengthens the hold of the internal vested interests. Equally, it will remain essentially a holding operation, again benefitting primarily the vested interests within, if this struggle, the struggle of any oppressed identity, is not articulated with *class struggle*, if it is conducted in oblivion of the economic structural contradictions of Indian society. For these contradictions, even as they determine the basic class oppressions in our society, also condition, most decisively, the working out of the identity-specific oppressions; and their resolution is a necessary, though by no means sufficient, condition for the elimination of these latter oppressions also. Such a resolution, however, calls for an united revolutionary movement of *all* oppressed and exploited people which is not possible without the requisite revolutionary consciousness among them. It should be obvious that it is impossible to develop such a consciousness without a prior and persistent critique of 'the identity-consciousness' which is in so many ways a much corrupted consciousness. All this applies with added force to religious identities for, by their very nature, here more than anywhere else, 'the tradition of all the dead generations weighs like a nightmare on the brain of the living', as Marx once put it in another context.

These general observations apart, in the context of communalism, there is one aspect of religious identity which requires specific mention. It is of the very nature of an identity that, in marking itself out as distinct or different, it divides itself from others. So does every religious identity. In fact all organised religion is essentially divisive of humankind, and more so for the high stakes involved, even if most of them are illusory. But important for the purpose of my argument is not this fact of community based, and in that sense, communal divisiveness, which is quite natural and obvious, and which may come to be fed, over time, by all sorts of other factors, including historically produced discriminations, contentions or antagonisms, and true or false perceptions of history and contemporary social reality. Really important is what happens to this divisiveness in specific historical contexts or conjunctures. Peaceful and coexistent, tolerant, accommodating and even fraternal in one context, it can become explosive and quite murderous in another. Notwithstanding cliches about religion being about love, and not hatred, or the loud mouthed *bhai bhai* business, history is witness to unparalleled intolerance, fighting, killing and hating, in the name of religion.* That is why we do not seek the basic cause of recent explosive emergence of communalism in religion or religious revivalism and fundamentalism, or in religious identities, their history or inherent divisiveness and its sundry ideological manifestations—though all these certainly feed or are manipulated to feed this communalism. We seek this cause in the concrete socio-historical context

* Always more honest than the many who invoke him or speak in his name, Gandhi recognised the grim fact of 'wars in the name of religion', and pointing out that 'these are not confined to Hindus and Mussalmans alone' wrote: 'The pages of world history are soiled with the bloody accounts of these religious wars.' But wedded as he was to a religious-idealist worldview, he did not have the slightest clue to the real historical causation of these wars. He could only urge upon us, once again, 'to discover an underlying unity among all religions' and insist: 'When you look at these religions as so many leaves of a tree they seem so different, but at the trunk they are one. 'Thus it has been before Gandhi and thus after him with the votaries of religion—their argumentation always has its quota of such Gandhi-like urging and insistence but, I may add, without Gandhi's honesty and sincerity and, above all, his abiding love and concern for the common Indian people.

and conjunctures of today, above all, in the economic and political matrix of contemporary India.**

This brings me to the important issue of the socio-economic matrix of India in its highly significant relation to contemporary communalism—and this matrix is the historically specific form of capitalist development in India.

**It is wrong to argue that 'the basic cause of communalism is cultural and psychological', or that 'communalism is above all a communal ideology...a false view,...a wrong understanding of reality'. Such arguments recognise an important aspect of the situation, which is yet a *secondary* aspect, and reduce the struggle against communalism to an educative, ideological-cultural exercise in which, while 'falsity' or 'evils' of communalism are exposed and appeals continue to be made in the name of 'true religion', it is propagation of secularism which comes to acquire decisive importance. This is certainly necessary and helpful, but hardly an adequate answer to the challenge of contemporary communalism.

In fact, secularism as propagated in India is not an adequate answer even to the problem of religion insofar as religion, in its diverse manifestation, is indeed an important issue in understanding and fighting communalism or securing secularism in the country. *Sarva dharma sambhava* is hardly secularism—it is far more a celebration of all kinds of religion and religiosity by the Indian state and in Indian politics and public life. The conventional liberal view, which would treat religion as 'a private affair', is a permissible tactical position, but only that—it evades all the real or difficult issues involved. Somewhat more genuine liberalism, which urges propagation of secularism as 'scientific temper', does in a way confront these issues but remains inadequate, for religion is not merely a set of false or erroneous ideas, just waiting to yield to a rational, scientific understanding of things! What is needed is a different, deeper understanding of religion, religious phenomena, religious ideologies and identities, as suggested in the text above. And, at the very least, secularism in Indian polity demands the rejection of every form of religion and religiosity in the conduct of the state, the working of its various institutions.

We need to notice its essential logic as a *capitalist* development. Just as, before 1947, the structural logic of British imperialism meant the accumulation of wealth in England and poverty in India, the structural logic of Indian capitalism is most manifest today, as already mentioned, in the creation of 'two nations' in this country in only 'forty years of freedom'. Its *historical specificity* has given it a strong lumpen or comprador character, presided over as it is by a bourgeoisie born old without ever having known youth, with none of the possible virtues of youth and all the vices of old age. Here all the evils of belated capitalist development, semi-feudalism, bureaucratised public sector and bloated bourgeois politics daily enter into and reinforce each other. Romesh Thapar once described it as 'some strange kind of corrupted capitalist growth', where; we might add in the words of Marx, 'we suffer not only from the living but from the dead' also.

Today, every aspect of social life in India bears the signature of this historically specific Indian form of capitalist development—its mark is there on our morality, our culture, our politics, on everything, everywhere. It is there, for example, on our 'national integration', or the so-called 'mainstream' which, bearing the impress of India's corrupt and corrupting, somewhat lumpen capitalist development, is increasingly a dirty mainstream—corrupt, communal and criminalised, a repressively homogenising mainstream. The fact to be deplored is not that we are not integrated but that we are intergrated the *capitalist* way, which has meant not only general exploitation and oppression of the people but also, and necessarily, an unequal and uneven development in the country, clearly visible, for example, in the emergence of 'two nations' in India and a certain 'internal colonialism' as well. Such 'integration' therefore carries within it strong disintegrative tendencies. It is not without reason that today, especially in the absence of a class-based people's politics, all the identities, all the divides and fissures of Indian society, including the religious, have simultaneously become significant and *explosive*.

What is more, Indian economic development with its structural logic of inequality and unevenness has produced not only 'two Indias' and an everwidening gulf between the two, with all its disintegrative consequences, but also, together, with poverty and hunger and heart-breaking inhuman conditions of life for the vast masses of our people, a society of myriad old and new oppressions, insecurities and alienations, with no jobs or ideals for its youth or vision and values for the people, a society in deep social and moral crisis indeed—*thus providing a continuing social-material basis for the production and reproduction, sustenance and reinforcement of all sorts of religiosity or 'dharmikta', revivalism, fundamentalism and obscurantism, and also ideologies and practices like communalism*. (Apropos 'the Punjab problem', for example, it is well to remember that the green revolution, as an integral part of Indian capitalist development, has meant not only 'economic growth' but also sharpened economic disparities, class divisions and social tensions. And in its progress it turned Punjab into a 'chicken- and- whisky land', giving rise to an extraordinary corruption and vulgarity of life and culture in the State. 'This, in the absence of a strong countervailing democratic or socialist culture, should explain a great deal about the compensatory appeal of religious fundamentalism, with its harking back to the puritanical traditions of early Sikhism, etc.)

Scholarship on communalism has certainly gained for us a great deal of 'retail sanity' about communalism in contemporary India. But given its strong empiricistic orientation, it has failed to see the 'wholesale madness' which has today come to characterise the Indian society as a whole—its economy, politics, ideology, culture and so on—in which communalism, an 'insanity' itself, has become explosively functional at the present historical conjuncture. And it has become so functional today, above all, by virtue of the politics practised by the Indian ruling classes through their diverse political formations in recent years. This is the last issue that I would like to deal with.

The Indian ruling classes have always found religion, religiosity or *dharmikta* most useful for reinforcing their hegemony, their ideological dominance and social control over the common people, making easier the latter's continued acceptance of an unjust and iniquitous social order. This usefulness has been well-secured through the typically Indian concept of secularism, defined as *sarva dharma sambhava* (equal respect for all religions), which is in fact no secularism at all—it is far more a celebration of all kinds of religion and religiosity, ignorance, obscurantism and social oppression. Also their political parties have never been averse to the exploitation of religion, or communalism, to a greater or lesser degree, in their struggle for power at different levels in the Indian state. *Sarva dharma sambhava* has in fact facilitated the accommodation or 'appeasement' of every sort of communal interest and politics, including the cultivation of communal vote banks.

But even as communalism as also religion and revivalism are there among the people and the Indian society continues to produce and reproduce these in a rich variety of form, expression and use; depending upon particular, historically specific causes and conjunctures*, *the most significant recent*

* Here is an illustration. Apropos 'Hindu chauvinism', in his introduction to *Anatomy of a Confrontation: The Babri Masjid-Ram Janmabhoomi Issue*, S. Gopal writes:

'Hindu chauvinism is an unsurprising counter to the Islamic fundamentalism that is spreading in India and various other parts of the world. Seeking to confront throw-backs to medievalism by modern secular attitudes is a difficult endeavour, far easier to *development* has been the shift of the Congress-I, the major political formation of the Indian ruling classes, to an openly communalist politics under the leadership of Indira Gandhi

---

take up similar, backward-looking postures in dealing with the menace. Also, just as the Jews were denounced in Nazi Germany as a threat to the economic prosperity of the nation as a whole, so in India Muslims are today being made the scapegoats of impending decline, particularly of retail and small-scale business, in the Indian countryside. In the riots in Kota in September 1989, those killed were mostly the Muslims who had been once poor but now roused envy because they had been enriched by money from the Gulf. Tamil Nadu has been relatively free of antagonism between Hindus and Muslims; but this record was tarnished by communal rioting in Madras city in September 1990, and it is said that Marwari traders rewarded the hooligans who burnt shops owned by Muslims. In the clashes in the Bhagalpur area in October 1990, not a single Muslim weaver family was spared in the Champanagar and Nathnagar localities, famous for their silk textile production. Nor is it without significance that many of the disputed religious sites constitute valuable urban property. The craving for plunder has not departed with Mahmud of Ghazni.

'Such economic greed, rivalry and exploitation draw sustenance from other sources as well. Fundamentalism is an umbrella providing shade to smuggling, drugpeddling and other dubious, anti social activities. Indians settled abroad, clinging to obscurantist versions of their religion in an effort to salvage their identity in an alien context, have thrown their weight—and funds—on the side of reaction in their home country...' etc.

Needless to add, the form, expression or use of minority communalism or chauvinism is subject to a similar historical specificity. And, the obviously important differences in their situation notwithstanding, the two communalisms regularly feed each other and are equally divisive and harmful to the interest of the common people everywhere, in every community. They need to be struggled against in an equally determined manner, with due recognition that if majority communalism is the greater danger, the minorities have a greater stake in the secular character of the Indian polity.

during her last phase and later of Rajiv Gandhi, the consequent emergence of state sponsored or condoned communalism, religious revivalism, superstition and obscurantism, particularly the varieties associated with the majority Hindu religion, and the growing identity of Hindu chauvinist ideology with Indian nationalism—all of which has been since, far more naturally, taken advantage of and reinforced by the other, openly communal ruling class political formation, the BJP. Obviously, it is here that the somewhat shaky Indian ruling classes have been seeking, through their different political formations, to a greater or lesser degree, a newer basis of hegemony for their class rule.

The heightening of communalism today is simultaneously the product of social, moral and political crisis in society and the response of the ruling classes to this crisis. With the older bases of their power and hegemony weakening, they are increasingly turning to communalism in general and to Hindu communalism in particular, to win votes, fragment and divide the people and, above all, secure their continued political and ideological dominance over them. Faced with a worsening economic situation for the people and mounting discontent, widespread violence, disruption and disorder in civil society, and their deepest-ever crisis of legitimacy since independence, the ruling classes are seeking increasingly authoritarian, even fascist, answers to their problems. It is in this overall context, essentially a context of classes and class struggle, open or hidden, actual or potential, that communalism as ideology and practice has become functional, more than ever before, in contemporary India.

This heightened importance of communalism in the politics of the Indian ruling classes may even betoken a certain weakness of character, almost a failure of nerve on their part. For while there are problems galore, an increasing loss of credibility and even significant revolutionary developments in certain parts of the country, there is as yet no real or present threat from below to their political power or class domination. If these ruling classes, or their political representatives, are yet betraying a strong tendency to scuttle even formal secularism for communalism and religious obscurantism, or, for that matter, even formal democracy for an increasingly authoritarian rule, this is indicative not only of a certain degeneration at the core of the Indian political system in recent years, but also of the feudal-colonial inheritance of the new rulers of India, of a certain comprador strain inherent in the character of the dominant sections of the Indian ruling classes, including the Indian bourgeoisie as a whole.

Let me state the issue in a slightly different, more specific manner. Following independence, throughout the Nehru era, what dominated the scene was politics of the ruling classes, as conducted by their political formations, the dominant Congress-I and the rest, more or less as a Hindu Undivided Family, on the basis of a working 'consensus', a balance of power and interests among them, the beneficiaries of the system as a whole. But after the economic crisis of the mid-sixties, and subject to the continuing constraints of the economic situation since then, this 'consensus' or 'balance' has been lost, the beneficiaries, ever more greedy and grasping, have been violating the rules of their own political game, inside the Parliament or state legislatures and outside —and 'democratic politics', insofar as it also provides a basis for the hegemony of the ruling classes and serves as an impersonal, non-arbitrary device for resolving their internal conflict of interests while articulating and promoting these interests as a whole, has been seriously undermined. Ruling class politics, especially because it faces, as yet, no significant revolutionary threat from below, has in fact increasingly acquired a no-holds-barred quality and with its corruption, criminality and lumpenism, its philandering ways and utter unscrupulousness, become a potent threat to Indian democracy as we have known it and a deadly exercise for our people, producing one tragedy after another for them. Here in this 'politicians' politics' (*la politique politicienne*) as Malraux once phrased it, it is truly the end justifying the means—any means, including the use of every form of religious revivalism, fundamentalism and obscurantism, and, of course, communalism.

Let me conclude with a tentative definition of contemporary communalism, even though a definition, at best, can be no more than barely suggestive of an understanding:

> Communalism in contemporary India, as ideology and practice, is above all an aspect of the politics of the ruling classes in a society with a massive feudal-colonial inheritance, deep religious divisions, and undergoing its own, historically specific form of capitalist development.

The understanding underlying this definition seeks to grasp communalism in all its complex interconnections, above all the more basic economic-structural and political interconnections that decisively condition the dynamics of contemporary communalism in the interrelated areas of personal life, politics, ideology, culture, etc. And the most important implication, the 'value slope' of this understanding, is that to be really effective the struggle against communalism has to be a struggle against *more* than communalism, just as a struggle for secularism has to be a struggle for *more* than only secularism in India. This struggle, even as it confronts communalism on its each and every specific terrain, has to be a part of our people's revolutionary struggle *against* the established order, the economy and politics of the ruling classes, and *for* an economically just and genuinely democratic social order in India, which in our times can only be socialism, or in more precise theoretical and historical terms, *a society in transition to socialism/communism*.

*Addenda**

On 'Hindu fascism'

It needs to be noticed that communalism is *an aspect*, and not the whole of even ruling class politics. Thus it is open to the impact of not only the inevitable shifts within this politics but also the ebb and flow of the country's politics in general, more particularly the people's struggle against communalism and against ruling class politics itself. Here, on the basis of our historical experience, it is possible to hazard the generalisation that the spread or heightening of communalism and related phenomena like religious revivalism, fundamentalism, or obscurantism, is in direct proportion to the depth of the crisis in Indian polity and politics of the ruling classes on the one hand and in inverse proportion to the presence or power of the Left or class-based people's politics on the other.

This generalisation, even as it indicates the correct path of struggle against communalism, is also suggestive of an entirely different kind of possibility. With the deepening socio-economic and moral crisis which has sharpened all the conflicts and contradictions within, and the increasing ineptitude of the rulers whose opportunist practice only ends up creating new problems while turning the old ones into running sores, Indian society and politics are steadily sliding into anarchy and authoritarian or mafia ways. In such a situation, communalism may well come to contribute to the rise of a specifically Indian form of fascism. Years ago Nehru

---

* Two excerpts from 'Communalism and the Struggle against Communalism: A Marxist View,' *Social Scientist*; Vol 18, nos. 8 9, August-September 1990.

had feared such a possibility and warned against it. Today the possibility is being recognised as a real threat by an increasing number of thoughtful people. We must not be alarmist about it but we do need to have a better understanding of such a possibility. For, almost invariably, this threatening authoritarianism is being misinterpreted: the concept which has gained currency in this regard is 'Hindu-fascism'; at other times it is 'Hindu communalism' which is spoken of as 'nascent' or 'impending' fascism in India.

Such conceptualisation or linguistic practice is not only misleading; it is also harmful to the cause of struggle against both communalism and the possible emergence of fascist authoritarianism in India.

At an obvious empirical level, 'Hindu fascism' as a concept ignores the role of communalism *as a whole* in the growing fascination of Indian society. This is not to deny 'the major threat' that comes from 'majority communalism', or the reality of discrimination the minorities suffer and the need to fight it, or their obviously greater stake in the secular character of Indian polity, etc, etc. But all this does not justify overlooking the very real contribution 'minority communalism' of various hues is making to the daily deteriorating situation in our country.

Furthermore, with its implicit treatment of Hindus as one undifferentiated mass, this concept virtually makes a gift of all those who regard themselves as Hindus to the communal politics of the ruling classes. It certainly makes it that much more difficult to help these Hindus understand—and vast masses of our poor and oppressed are among them—not only that Hinduism, like any other religion today, has no answers to the myriad problems they daily face and share with the rest of the common Indian people, but also that, if and when such a fascism arrives, while it will certainly mean an added oppression for the minorities, they, as Hindus, will not be its beneficiaries—they too will be, like most other ordinary

Indians, its victims, only their number, as Hindus, will be the largest among them.

It should also not be forgotten that if there will be something 'Hindu' about Indian fascism, it is likely to have a great deal more of 'nationalism' about it to give it the necessary thrust and legitimacy. Not 'Hindu communalism' but Hinduised nationalism is going to be part of its ideological mask. In our times fascism has often arrived in a typical alliance with chauvinistic nationalism of one kind or the other, and there is no dearth of such nationalism in our country today. Its rhetoric has already become almost unbearable. To speak of 'Hindu fascism' is to prevent recognition of this extremely significant ideological dimension of the developing fascisation of life and politics in contemporary India.

The most important problem with this concept however is that, utterly empiricist in registering what is apparent or most visible, it misses out on all the significant interconnections involved and has no explanatory value at all. Privileging 'Hindu communalism' for almost exclusive attention or analysis, as fact, ideology or whatever, it completely obscures what is most important in under-standing or explaining any possible rise of fascism in India—its class-basis, the system of class relations within which it is likely to develop and function, the class role it will be called upon to perform, etc. etc. As a product of the crisis in Indian polity and ruling class politics, fascism in India, whenever it comes and whatever the ideological mask, will be another, explicitly authoritarian, form of the rule of the dominant, exploiting classes, just as, in another setting 'democratic secular' is the preferred form. It will be a new method to realise the old policies, centered on maintaining the existing oppressive and exploitative economic and social structures of Indian society. The concept of 'Hindu fascism' simply fails to grasp this vital truth.

Needless to add, such a denouement of ruling class politics in India would indeed be a tragedy for the Indian people—the worst in a long list so far. It needs to be opposed and fought against by all means and at all costs. It can and must be averted.

But the beginning of wisdom and the possibility of a successful fight here, as in the fight against communalism, lies in recognising that, especially in recent years, the ruling class-politics, while preserving the organised structures of exploitation and oppression in India, has been producing only tragedies for the Indian people. Punjab, and now Kashmir are only the most obvious examples—there are and *shall be* many more. It is time we are 'nationalist' or 'patriotic' enough to have more faith in our own ruling classes. Today they are fully self-reliant— they can produce all the tragedies they need for the Indian people by themselves. They don't have to depend upon others, any foreign helping hands—not for this at any rate.

On 'Identitarianism'

Problems arising out of India's characteristic diversity or plurality need not detain us here. But our presumed concern with revolutionary politics persuades me to digress a little beyond what I have already stated, and make one implication of my argument more explicit. This is related to two interesting shifts of thought and action that occurred on the right and the left of the Indian political spectrum in the early eighties as a result of the continuing crisis in Indian politics in recent years. That the shifts have almost ended up as two escape routes does not take away from their significance, though it is only the issues raised by the shift on the left which concern us here.

On the right, among the liberals and not a few 'Gandhians', there was widespread disenchantment with the working of conventional party-based bourgeois politics, presided over, most of the time, by Congress(I), the: major political formation of the Indian ruling classes. Many felt betrayed and were indeed heart-broken at the way the Indian state had let them down—it had simply failed to deliver 'as an instrument of social transformation and equity', as, they believed, the democratic state in the West had done. Quite a few of them, therefore, sought salvation elsewhere—and found it, even if somewhat ambiguously, in the alternative of then emerging 'grass roots movements', in the work of 'new instrumentalities' like voluntary activism or what came to be described as 'non-party political formations'. This however, did not work out as expected, if for no other reason than that it was too narrow and fractured a base; ideologically as well as organisationally, to provide for any kind of alternative politics—liberal, left or any other. This is not to deny the significance of 'the emergence of these' formations' or the commendable work done by them in the cause of the people. One even hopes that the best of them will yet find their way, sooner rather than later, to a radical, if not revolutionary, practice of politics. But for the present their limitations of theory and practice are only too obvious.

I cannot pursue this subject here; except to report that, while these 'formations' continue to struggle to realise their possibilities, and interest in the 'escape route' persists, our liberals and 'Gandhians' are back with the Indian state, which they had in fact never really abandoned—hopefully content, for the time being at least, with the alternative politics of the National Front, another political formation of the Indian ruling classes.

It is the parallel shift on the left, however, which is of immediate interest to us. The disenchantment here was with the outcome of conventional class-politics as practised by the established communist parties, which had long lost its way in the mire of 'economism' and much of the working class itself to the ruling class politics. Quite a few of the radicals too, therefore, sought salvation elsewhere—and found it in the emerging, highly visible struggles of the long oppressed and more disadvantaged sections of the Indian people, 'identities' as they came to be called: minor nationalities or ethnic groups, religious minorities, dalits, tribals, women, and so on, all impelled to action by an iniquitous economic development, all struggling against an oppressive, homogenizing Indian state and India's equally oppressive social structures, and all of them seeking their rights and a place of dignity and honour among the Indian people. This shift of thought and action to the terrain of the struggles of these 'identities' too has not fared well—it can hardly claim to have significantly advanced the cause of left politics or revolutionary change in India. Nor is it likely to do so in future. In view of the limited and uncritical manner in which those involved in this shift have thought and acted in the matter of these identities and their struggles, it is only turning out to be an escape route on the left.

There is no doubt about the reality of injustice or grievances here, often long denied or neglected for being rooted deep in history; the groups or identities concerned are in fact victims of double oppression, and worse as in case of women—the class oppression which affects the exploited everywhere and the oppressions specific to each group or identity. These struggles are therefore most justified, they are a part of Indian peoples' struggle for a more just and humane social order. But in endorsing these struggles sharing in them or leading them, there is no justification for a simplistic, idealising or myth-making attitude towards these groups or identities, an attitude not uncommon with the left when speaking of 'the people' or 'the oppressed' (to say nothing of 'the proletariat' in another context). A form of *community*, historically constituted and evolving, an identity as such is not something sacred, a value in itself—its real life situation may have all kinds of negative, ugly features *within* that limit or diminish human beings, struggle, against which has to be a part of the larger struggle *without* .... Of decisive importance is the need to articulate this larger struggle with class struggle, to conduct it in full recognition of the economic-structural contradictions of Indian society. For these contradictions even as they determine the basic class oppressions in our society also condition, most decisively, the working out of the identity specific oppressions, and their resolution is a necessary, though by no means sufficient, condition for the elimination of these oppressions also. Such a resolution, however, calls for an united revolutionary movement of *all* oppressed people, which is not possible without requisite revolutionary consciousness among them. It should be obvious that it is impossible to develop such a consciousness without a prior and persistent critique of 'the identity-consciousness' which is, in the very nature of things, a much corrupted consciousness.

All this points to the implication I am wanting to make explicit, namely, the imperative need to infuse the aforementioned struggles in every way and everywhere with *socialist* concerns and articulate them, in theory as well as practice, with revolutionary class struggle, with a class-based people's politics. Such has always been the principle in Marxism for the conduct of such or similar struggles. It remains very much valid even today.

In needs to be emphasised that many things which the old communists did not do, or did badly, or have stopped doing; have still to be done by those who, coming after them, would develop a people's movement for a revolutionary break in our society. And class politics is one of those things, asking for a genuine *Marxist* practice. Unless this is done, the ongoing struggles of these groups or identities are likely to divide the oppressed even more, distort or corrupt their consciousness still further, and end up serving the interests of not the common people but the exploiting and other elite elements within, who ate only too eager to find a place for themselves in India's underdeveloped capitalism and over-developed bourgeois politics.